HELPING THE VICTIM

A Treatment Manual

RAPE
HELPING THE VICTIM

A Treatment Manual

by Susan Halpern

Dorothy J. Hicks, M.D.
CONSULTING EDITOR

Theresa L. Crenshaw, M.D.
CONTRIBUTING EDITOR

Medical Economics Company Book Division
Oradell, New Jersey 07649

Design by JoAnne Cassella

ISBN 0-87489-010-1

Medical Economics Company
Oradell, New Jersey 07649

Printed in the United States of America

First Printing   April, 1978
Second Printing   January, 1980

Contents

Foreword

This book is exactly what it says it is, a treatment manual, but one so well executed that it belongs in every rape-treatment center and in the hands of everyone dealing with sexual-assault victims.

The author has covered all aspects—from false suppositions about rape and rape victims to the long-term follow-up care of the patient. Examples of treatment protocols that the author gives are especially helpful.

The sections on police and criminal-justice system procedures are valuable because most laymen have had little or no experience with police, prosecutors and criminal courts.

The chapter on emotional first aid for "significant others" in the victim's life is a necessary part of the whole. Few people know the importance of the victim's peripheral support system. Without it, she may never recover fully.

The child-victim treatment recommendations have particular merit because the information is not readily available elsewhere. In our center, 30 per cent of the victims are under the age of 15, and similar statistics probably apply to other parts of the country. Child abuse is a problem that, like sexual assault, has only recently come into prominence. Law-enforcement officials estimate at least 500,000 cases of child abuse in the U.S. every year.

I endorse this book as comprehensive, readable, understandable, usable. I wish we had had such a guide in 1974 when Jackson Memorial Hospital's Rape Treatment Center was established.

Let me repeat: This manual is an essential tool for all agencies and individuals concerned with the crime of sexual assault and effective treatment for victims.

Dorothy J. Hicks, M.D.
Rape Treatment Center
Jackson Memorial Hospital
University of Miami School of Medicine
Miami, Fla.

Preface

Rape can be devastating, dehumanizing and brutal. History records it as part of the human scene, accompanied by such myths as: Women enjoy and invite rape. When there's no resistance, there's no rape. Or, to quote an 18th-century lawmaker: "And it hath been said by some to be no rape to force a woman who conceives at the time; for it is said, that if she had not consented, she could not have conceived."

Males as well as females are violated, but for simplicity I refer to the victim as "she."

There are no exact figures on rape victims. Still, "FBI statistics confirm that rape is the fastest growing . . . [but] probably one of the most underreported crimes in the United States today," according to Dr. Elaine Hilberman, author of *The Rape Victim*.

While the actual number of victims likely will remain unknown, the effect of rape on the victim has become clearer. She can suffer from the crime's physical, psychological, social and legal implications. Moreover, though medical/law enforcement facilities are presumed to help her, they often contribute instead to her anguish. Their unsympathetic or judgmental response makes her feel more the accused than the accuser.

The rape victim needs help from enlightened physicians, nurses, social workers, hospital administrators, police, prosecutors and community-minded citizens. This manual is dedicated to them.

Susan Halpern

Publisher's notes

This book is the direct outcome of Susan Halpern's working experiences with the New York City Mayor's Task Force on Rape, as well as the Queens (N.Y.) Hospital Center's patient-representative office and emergency room. The author also has been affiliated with the New York City Addiction Services Agency and has written a book on drug abuse.

Dorothy Jane Hicks, M.D., is an associate professor in the Department of Obstetrics and Gynecology at the University of Miami School of Medicine, Miami. She is a member of the active attending staffs of Jackson Memorial Hospital, University of Miami Hospitals and Clinics (National Children's Cardiac Hospital), Cedars of Lebanon Hospital and Broward General Hospital. Dr. Hicks has been the medical director of Jackson Memorial Hospital's Rape Treatment Center since its inception. A list of her activities, published works and memberships would fill several pages. In addition, she is frequently invited to lecture via professional and public media on sexual assault and its consequences.

Theresa L. Crenshaw, M.D., is clinical instructor, Department of Reproductive Medicine, University of California Medical School, San Diego, and codirector of The Crenshaw Clinic. The clinic treats sexual and related problems, about which Dr. Crenshaw has written extensively. She is a fellow of the Reproductive Biology Research Foundation; part of its training includes a year with William H. Masters, M.D., and Virginia E. Johnson. Dr. Crenshaw is also cochairperson of the Western Region of the American Association of Sex Educators, Counselors and Therapists (AASECT).

Because fewer males than females are sexually assaulted, this manual emphasizes female treatment, as recommended by three women. But no bias or female chauvinism is involved. Following the manual's suggestions will, in fact, help ensure that innocent men are not convicted of the crime of rape.

How to use this manual

The first chapter deals with rape myths, and why they are myths rather than facts. Chapter 13, written especially for this manual by Dr. Theresa L. Crenshaw, offers tips on counseling of rape victims' families and friends. The final chapter suggests how agencies and individuals within a community can pull together to provide effective victim treatment. The Appendix contains helpful forms, charts and related articles from various sources.

But between beginning and end are chapters addressed to agencies or to stages of rape-victim care. Separately and together, they will facilitate health- and legal-care providers' jobs. The chapters give prefatory and sometimes concluding remarks with interspersed step-by-step procedures. This format should simplify manual use.

The book integrates its treatment of victim needs with a description of health and legal services that are generally available. Of course, all institutions have limitations. Recommendations for expanded services therefore are supplied, not as rigid formulae but as easily adaptable ideas.

CHAPTER 1

Debunking the myths

Real help for the rape victim starts with clearing the mind of some old misconceptions. One basic myth, for example, is that if a woman resists, she can't be raped. The corollary: Good women don't get raped.

There's no conclusive evidence on the efficacy of resistance to rape. Resistance may prevent some sexual assaults, but can lead to increased brutality, or even rape-homicides. It is important to note the circumstances that make it dangerous for the victim to resist—the greater size or strength of the assailant, the presence of a weapon or the number of attackers.

The victim may believe that her only alternative to submission is death. But those who submit and consequently show little or no sign of physical trauma are judged as somehow guilty, even though submission does not necessarily imply consent. Another issue involved concerns the definition of femininity, which is equated with passivity in our culture. Female socialization emphasizes learned helplessness; little girls are seldom taught to be assertive or aggressive. A female socialized in this way is hardly prepared to resist sexual attack. Even when women are taught self-defense as adults, they often lack the strength, quick reflexes or combative mental attitude needed to ward off such assaults.

A second myth hinges on the she-got-what-she-deserved notion and blames the victim's dress (suggestive), behavior (provocative) or whereabouts (a bar or rough neighbor-

1

hood). This shifts the blame from attacker to victim. That he initiated the violence is ignored.

This myth says that rape was precipitated by the victim's nonverbal messages. If, for example, she wore shorts, the man interpreted her clothing as an invitation to make sexual advances. If, in addition, she thumbed a ride, rape was "only what she asked for," claim her critics.

But for many modern females, shorts are an acceptable style of dress. Society *does* sanction and encourage "looking good." Further, hitching rides is a not uncommon method of transportation today, part of a life style that the young are comfortable with.

Unwritten rules that are part of archaic social/sexual structures do not permit women the freedom to do as they please. They are supposed to have male or societal protection, whether they want it or not. They're called "fair game" if they go out alone at night or visit a bar. Women who want to be independent and engage in such activities risk rape. But so do other women.

Another myth is built on sexual fantasies women are believed to have. These fantasies involve their seduction and submission (related to the passive role that culture has attributed to women). Or so some men would like to believe. It's true that this kind of fantasizing does occur, but usually within the bounds of consensual sexual activity that implies sex without worry of violating one's own or the partner's integrity. The sexual partner (seducer) is seen as desirable, and the experience is viewed as pleasurable.

Rape, however, is an act of forced sexual intercourse against the victim's will. It degrades and humiliates. No woman wants that.

The fourth myth: Women cry "rape" out of anger or to cover up an embarrassing situation; they do it all the time.

Government statistics suggest that only one out of five rapes is reported. Though this estimate's accuracy can't be tested, crisis-center counselors note that many women will

2

not report rape to the police or go to a hospital for treatment. Others hide childhood episodes of sexual assault until much later in their lives.

Reasons for the reluctance are valid: humiliation, fear of the rape stigma, judgmental treatment by medical and legal authorities, fear of causing difficulties and disruptions in the family.

For various reasons, some women have unjustly accused men of rape, but the number is much smaller than a male-dominated society accepts. In addition, although false charges occur for many crimes, only in rape cases is it assumed that the criminal justice system will be unable to protect the defendant against a lying plaintiff.

Whether you operate on myths or facts, however, the fact remains that if you or a loved one were raped, you'd want the best possible treatment to be provided.

Debunking the myths

CHAPTER 2

Immediate needs

Medical treatment is usually a victim's most urgent need. But immediately and after, she'll be affected as much by the attitudes of those who respond as by the treatment they give her. Whoever is first contacted—the Good Samaritan who happens to come by, a police officer, private or emergency-room physician or hospital admissions clerk—must be careful to provide nonjudgmental support. It will have the dual result of calming the victim and helping her decide her medical/legal desires and requirements.

1. Avoid impersonal, tactless or hostile remarks. A victim is particularly sensitive to negative attitudes born of sexual myths. In fact, part of her distress and part of the hostility you may feel stem from that social conditioning.

2. Assume she is telling the truth. She's entitled to no less than the individual who claims robbery: Both are considered innocent victims. Believe her even if she's dressed outrageously, is an admitted prostitute or has gone home to bathe and clean up before seeking help.

3. If severe trauma (bleeding, lacerations, gunshot or knife wounds) is present, telephone the local emergency number. Even if severe trauma is not evident, encourage her to seek medical attention. Hospital personnel should arrange for ambulance pickup. Do not move the victim.

4. If possible, have the victim make the call to doc-

tor, hospital, friend or relative. If she cannot, call for her in her presence after first discussing what she wants revealed, and to whom.

5. Advise the victim not to wash or change her clothing. Make her as comfortable as possible while waiting for medical or police attention.

6. If a police car or ambulance is not immediately available and the victim is ambulatory, help her arrange transportation to a hospital or doctor.

7. Offer to stay with her or accompany her to the selected facility. Fear of being alone is common after an assault.

8. Do not ask probing questions about the assault, yet allow her to talk about it if she wishes.

9. Do not point out safety precautions you feel she should have taken. They may trigger unnecessary guilt. Further, for many victims, precautions would not have prevented the attack.

10. If you receive the victim's call at the local police station, hospital or crisis center, and she seems to need ongoing reassurance, stay on the phone with her until help arrives.

11. If the victim is at or near the scene of the assault, tell her that she should not alter it in any way.

12. Remember that, in the past, the ordinary response to a rape victim was disbelieving and judgmental. The result: unsympathetic, unsupportive or less than adequate care for her.

Rape victims are in *crisis*—a word used throughout this manual to mean reaction to a highly stressful situation that may initially cause shock, loss of self-esteem or change in self-perception and decreased ability to function or make responsible decisions.

These emotional needs must be recognized and met.

CHAPTER 3

Arrival at the emergency room

Hospital emergency rooms, the principal treatment sites for most rape victims, can provide physical and psychological aid—or simply increase distress. Because they play such pivotal roles in victim care, emergency rooms are being pressured now to humanize their approach toward sexual-assault victims. They differ from other noncritical emergency-room cases in that they have been emotionally traumatized, even if not hurt physically.

1. Give rape victims priority over all nonemergency patients. Several large hospitals have devised systems that alert medical or gynecological residents to give immediate treatment to rape victims.

2. In the case of a child or teen-age victim, call the pediatrics department.

3. Have registration staff members participate in in-service rape treatment courses. Frequently, patients do not identify themselves as rape victims but ask, instead, to see a gynecologist or say they have "a problem." Sensitivity and training will enable staff members to perceive the real problem.

4. If possible, bypass registration procedures, but have a registration staff member escort the victim to a special waiting area or examining room.

5. Ensure as much privacy for the victim as possible. She may be in shock or in pain. And her clothing may be soiled and torn. Under no circumstances should she be expected to sit in the common wait-

ing room, embarrassed and ignored for hours.

6. If one room cannot be set aside permanently for the purpose, find an area such as an unused examination room or an office (generally unoccupied during evening hours when most assaults take place) that offers temporary privacy and quiet. Quiet especially calms the victim of an assault and may encourage her to discuss her plight.
7. Never call the victim "the rape." She should be addressed and referred to as Miss, Mrs. or Ms.
8. Offer the services of an on-premises counselor, or one provided by a local rape-crisis center. Make sure counseling services are available even during late evening or early dawn hours.
9. If there is a delay, explain the reasons.
10. Never leave the victim alone.
11. Tell the victim whether the hospital charges for examination and other services. If it does, and the victim wishes to go to another hospital, give her a list of appropriate institutions.
12. Never turn the victim away without helping her obtain medical aid.

Reimbursement of hospital costs

An important hospital function in rape cases is the collection of evidence. It is necessary for successful prosecution. Accordingly, some experts believe that county/municipal funds should be used to cover evidence-collection charges, as well as hospital examination and laboratory costs.

In Illinois, state law requires hospitals to provide comprehensive care: examination, evidence collection, tests, medication and counseling. All expenses are paid for by the State Department of Health.

Somewhat similarly, New Jersey law calls for absorption of a rape victim's hospital costs by the county, though she is obliged to submit a claim to the Violent Crime Compensation Board. Other states have this kind of bureau, too. Unfortunately, none of them guarantees that the victim will be reimbursed.

The state attorney's office pays hospital expenses in one Maryland county. In others, they are paid for with money funneled through the police department.

Hospitals in some cities (Cleveland, Philadelphia, Denver, Louisville and Washington, D.C., for example) offer free care to rape victims, generally absorbing the cost in overall hospital operating expenses. In San Diego, evidence-collection costs are covered, but medical care and VD/pregnancy tests are not.

There is insurance coverage for some victims. Those with "accidental injury" coverage can be reimbursed, since rape is indeed accidental injury, says The Health Insurance Institute. Psychiatric counseling expenses are covered only if the victim's policy contains that clause. Many victims will not take advantage of either coverage because they do not want to reveal the rape to insurers.

Arrival at the emergency room

9

CHAPTER 4

Medical history

Preparing a medical history for a rape victim is not easy. First, the victim is likely to be reluctant to discuss the experience. Second, medical *and* legal ramifications of sexual-assault cases must be kept in mind by the physician or nurse who takes the history. And finally, that individual—perhaps more than others—must make the most of the opportunity to put the victim at ease and win her trust. The following steps will help:

1. Allow the victim the dignity of sitting, covered, during the history.
2. Introduce yourself and address the victim by proper name (never "Dear" or "Honey," no matter how young she may be).
3. Permit a relative or friend to remain during the history, but exclude angry or upset parents. They communicate their distress to the victim, making the situation more difficult. In such cases, call in a crisis-intervention counselor.
4. Explain briefly that the history is necessary to assess trauma and treatment, in conformity with hospital and legal requirements.
5. Never indicate by expression or word that the event's details are shocking or repulsive. A reassuring "Yes, that's happened before" will help minimize the victim's embarrassment.
6. Write legibly. Subpoenaed medical records are too often nearly or totally illegible, causing delay

and frustration for the prosecutor and the victim.

7. Take a complete and accurate history. If there's a discrepancy between the victim's testimony and the medical record, the latter will be considered the correct version. "It does not seem to occur to people . . . that the record might be carelessly written. Any hospital error in recording can be held against the victim," say Burgess and Holmstrom who have written a book on the rape victim (see bibliography in the Appendix). On the other hand, only major history points are covered at some clinics. Their staffs believe that a victim, confused and agitated when first seen, may give inaccurate information that later conflicts with the history taken by the police.

8. Be sure to get the following information:
   — Victim's name, age, address, phone number.
   — Time of attack.
   — Time of examination.
   — Is she sore/bleeding/in pain?
   — Has she douched/washed/urinated/defecated since the assault?
   — Has she changed clothes?
   — When did she have her last menstrual period?
   — Is she past childbearing age?
   — Is a prior conception possible?
   — What kind of birth-control method, if any, does she use?
   — Has she had a hysterectomy or tubal ligation?
   — Does she have any known allergies?
   — Is she taking any medication?
   — Did vaginal/anal/oral intercourse take place?
   — Were any foreign objects used?
   — Did the assailant hit her or use force? Some blows to the body do not result in immediately visible bruises. (Consider having the victim

return in a few days if bruise discoloration develops. Then the bruises can be documented by photographs.)

9. Avoid open-ended questions such as "What happened?" and phrases that imply that the victim initiated the act. For example, "Did the assailant put his penis in your mouth?" is preferable to "Did you have oral sex with the assailant?"
10. Tell the victim she need relate only those facts that will aid the physician in his examination.
11. Record what she relates in her own words, putting quotation marks around them. Go back later to fill in missing information.
12. If possible, take down her report in an unbroken narrative.

Medical history

Legal aspects to consider:
1. A victim has the right to prosecute her assailant.
2. If she brings her case to court, corroborative evidence (history, examination findings and laboratory analyses) may be subpoenaed.
3. The medical history must contain information on physical findings, treatment rendered or recommended and evidence collected.
4. The medical history records *observations* of the examiner, not conclusions. A typical observation, acceptable in court, is: "There was considerable laceration of outer labia, and bruises on both inner thighs; her underpants were stained and torn."
5. The medical history does not offer an opinion on whether the victim was raped. The history records only whether medical evidence indicates recent sexual intercourse and/or the use of force.
6. The word "rape," strictly a legal term, may not appear as a medical diagnosis in the history. "Alleged rape" and "alleged sexual assault" are the

correct terms to use. Unfortunately, however, their use does give the impression that the victim's word is in doubt. One way to avoid that impression is to write: ''The victim says she was sexually assaulted.''

Medical history

CHAPTER 5

Medical examination

Pelvic examination resembles the rape victim's earlier traumatic experience. The same organs are touched. The same lack of dignity and control over the situation prevails. Even the commands may be similar. To help minimize the victim's distress, the examining physician should:

1. Examine the victim privately. In teaching hospitals, rape victims should not be used for instructional purposes. Exclude other patients and police officers. If the victim requests it, however, allow the presence of a female counselor, friend or relative during the examination. Before or after, do not leave the victim alone in the examining room.

2. Explain what the examination will entail, and what sensations she may feel. Use words such as, "You may be a little nervous, so let me tell you what I'm going to do." Give instructions tactfully. For example, do not say, "Lie down and spread your legs." Instead, ask her to change into a gown, sit on the table, then lie back and let her legs separate naturally.

3. Although the patient can assume the dorsal position by herself or with the nurse's aid, help her to move to the head of the table and gain the lying position. This kind of physician contact has psychological benefits.

4. Talk to her throughout the procedure. Explain what you are finding, especially if findings are

15

reassuring. Ask if she is aware of sore areas, cuts or other wounds. If the victim is in shock or otherwise unable to answer, her expression may reveal pain or discomfort.

5. Maintain eye contact (a pillow for the victim's head helps). Comments directed to the nurse make the patient feel like a mere object—again. The bimanual exam can be accomplished standing next to her. During other procedures, lift your head periodically to talk to the victim.

6. Examine external genitalia for abrasions, cuts, semen or seminal fluid, dried matter, other foreign matter, swellings or lice. Pay special attention to the vulva, perineal areas and inner thighs. Examine the mouth for lacerations, broken or loose teeth and bruised gums.

7. Check especially for signs of force. Some states have eliminated the corroboration rule, but juries still look for medical evidence to substantiate a rape claim. Signs and symptoms of force are considered such evidence and must be described accurately. They include: cigarette burn marks; rope burns; knife wounds; fractures; scratches on legs, back, arms, breasts and elsewhere; broken fingernails; teeth marks and bruises, especially on breasts and inner thighs; and blackened eyes. As signs of first intercourse, look for superficial tears in the mucosa of the vulva below the hymen, and in the posterior fourchette.

8. For the internal exam, use a speculum moistened with warm water (lubricating jelly will invalidate the forensic tests) to minimize the shock of cold steel touching the vagina. If the area is sore, the sensation is worse. Look for signs of damage to vaginal walls, cervix and fornix areas, lacerations and possible hemorrhage. Take a Pap smear. The

cytologist may find sperm in it, if he is asked to check. And taking a Pap smear is good medicine.

9. Before the bimanual exam, help the victim to relax. The vaginal entrance tightens in women who are tense about the procedure, which can then become painful. But merely telling the victim to relax is meaningless. Instead, ask her to breathe slowly and deeply for a few minutes. Tell her the muscles to be relaxed are those used to hold in a bowel movement. Warn her she may feel she is about to urinate, but that she will not. Also say she

Who should examine the victim?

A resident or attending physician specializing in gynecology—or pediatrics, in the case of a child victim—is the best of all choices for rape examination and treatment.

Less desirable are the services of emergency-room doctors who are short on time and, perhaps, experience with rape victims. Some hospitals without an OB/gyn department have found that using specially trained emergency-room physicians is satisfactory. A Florida hospital without an OB/gyn section has another answer to the problem. It retains a number of private gynecologists on an on-call, rotation basis. They are paid through the county commissioner's office.

It is the general opinion of experts that rape examination and treatment should not be performed by interns because they lack experience, and may rotate quickly out of the emergency room and thus be unavailable for a court appearance.

However, one medical expert says the overriding consideration is that the physician be trained, willing and compassionate. No one would argue with that.

may feel a little pain. If she knows what to expect, she'll be less anxious.

10. If a rectal exam is necessary, explain the procedure first. It is unpleasant, and the victim should be told so. Also tell her that she may feel as though she is about to have a bowel movement, but that she will not.

11. Treat all traumatized areas, using a local anesthetic to repair vaginal wounds. A tampon in place at the time of the rape may have been pushed far back into the vaginal cavity and require removal. Save the tampon for evidence; sperm may be recovered from it.

12. After examination and treatment and when the victim has assumed a comfortable sitting position:
   — Advise her of possible reactions from the rape: vaginal irritation, discharge or itching and, possibly, headaches. Oral sex may cause sore throat or difficulty in swallowing. Anal sex may result in rectal pain, soreness or bleeding. Pain around neck or thighs may occur from the uncomfortable, forced position during rape.
   — If the victim's emotional state warrants it, prescribe sleeping pills, but not tranquilizers.
   — Administer tetanus toxoid, if indicated.
   — Carefully record all traumatized areas and treatment rendered. Use an androgenous diagram of the body to note trauma areas. Use diagrams of the genital region to note genital trauma.
   — SIGN ALL MEDICAL RECORDS.

Examination of a child
The very young victim presents a particularly sensitive and difficult case. Some youngsters are sexually abused in the

course of general child abuse. If incest or injury by a relative or family friend occurred, obtaining information from the child or family may be virtually impossible. Children exposed to violence or excessive parental reaction will be additionally fearful and upset. Nurses and physicians may find the following suggestions helpful in minimizing the child's physical and emotional trauma:

1. Speak to and touch the victim gently. Talk slowly, and explain that she is being examined because of possible injury.

2. If one parent has a calming, supportive effect on the child, allow him or her to be present during the examination. However, it is too painful for some parents to watch, while others who are hysterical or angry make it more traumatic.

3. Try to assess damage by visual examination alone, under good lighting. If it appears that an internal examination is necessary, give the child a general anesthetic or mild sedative.

4. Use special instruments for the internal examination: otoscopes, medicine dropper to aspirate, special vaginoscopes, nasal speculum, cystoscopes and miniature panendoscopes.

5. Repair lacerations, under anesthesia, with atraumatic, absorbent sutures. Use a small needle and fine catgut. If an adult needle is used, introitus size can be reduced. The most usual injury in raped female children is a midline tear to the anus and rectal mucosa, and sometimes periurethral damage. There are occasional vaginal ruptures.

6. As with adult patients, record findings and treatment rendered, and sign all medical records.

Medical examination

19

CHAPTER 6

Evidence collection

Few physicians are trained to collect evidence, by legal definition, but it is an integral part of a rape victim's examination, and can make or break her case against the assailant.

The following steps will help the physician in proper evidence collection:

1. Place all evidence in appropriate containers. Label each with victim's name, the date, anatomical location of evidence (if applicable) and the examining physician's name.

2. Examine outer and inner garments. Look for rips and blood or stains from seminal fluid, especially on underpants. Semen stains on clothing appear as off-white or yellowish shiny spots. Place bits of sand, mud, grass, hair and other matter in an envelope.

3. Place stained garments in separate paper bags (plastic breeds bacteria that decompose the evidence). Have family or friend bring replacements, or offer suitable garments from hospital supply. The examination sheet may contain blood or semen stains. Place it in a separate paper bag, too.

4. If the victim was assaulted vaginally and has not bathed, comb the pubic area, and cut a few pubic hairs and any matted hair. Place cuttings and combings in separate envelopes.

5. If victim scratched the assailant, her fingernails

21

may contain blood or tissue. Cut the fingernails and place them in an envelope.

6. Examine the victim's body for blood or semen stains. Remove stains by rolling a saline-dampened swab over the area.

7. Obtain material from the vulva, vagina, urethra and cervix (material from the cervix is especially important because sperm—significant where little or no physical trauma took place—lives longest there) by aspirating fluid from the areas, if possible, or use a swab or plastic spoon or spatula. A child's or a dry adult vagina may be washed with saline solution before aspirating or swabbing. A 2-cc saline solution is not likely to dilute the resulting evidence.

8. Immediately prepare a wet mount from aspirate or swab, and examine it for the presence of motile or nonmotile sperm. Note that absence of sperm does not necessarily indicate nonintercourse; the assailant may have failed to ejaculate, may have had a vasectomy or be aspermic. In recording results, use correct phraseology, such as, "Microscopic examination revealed (did not reveal) presence of . . ." Do not write, "Nothing found."

9. Prepare a slide of the aspirated or swabbed material, air-dry but do not fix it. It is needed for the laboratory semen test. Label the slide by etching with a diamond-tipped pencil.

10. Place aspirated fluid or the swab in a test tube for other lab tests.*

*Acid phosphatase tests are sometimes performed to screen for the presence of human semen, though they are not everywhere considered conclusive evidence of rape.

The blood group antigen test can be used to classify a semen stain in factors equivalent to human blood types, but only if the assailant is a secretor (and not everyone is). That can be established by a saliva sample, but since it may be difficult to obtain and because of other limitations, the test is not routinely performed.

Other semen components—corpora amylacea, spermine and choline—break down quickly or may be found in other parts of the body. Thus, positive test results based on these components must be qualified by experts, creating still another (unwanted) step in evidence collection and explanation.

11. Swab oral or rectal areas, if appropriate. Place swabs in separate stoppered test tubes.
12. In cases involving severe trauma, have a female nurse or female police officer take photographs, according to arrangements with the police department. Victim consent is necessary, for emotional as well as legal reasons. One New York City hospital gynecologist makes duplicate color photographs of stained clothing and obvious lacerations, with the hospital keeping one copy.

Whatever evidence may be gathered from victims of sexual assault within a legal jurisdiction is carefully kept on file (for periods that vary according to local requirements) for two reasons: The victim may be unable to decide immediately whether to prosecute. The assailant may be caught long after the medical examination.

Evidence collection kit

Procedure is simplified by use of a prepared evidence collection kit or set of supplies. Many are available from commercial sources. However, it's not difficult to assemble the necessary items and keep them ready in the OB/gyn or pediatric examining room cabinet. One kit put together by a Texas hospital contains:

Four slides	Six cotton-tipped swabs
Disposable plastic comb	Spray can of cytological fixative
Three stoppered test tubes	Information booklet for victim
Diamond-tipped pencil	Syringes
Medical form	Paper envelopes
Paper bags	Instruction sheet

Therefore, after collection, the physician or institution must maintain rigid control of the evidence. Control should include mechanisms for retaining labeled evidence and transfering it between physician/hospital, police department and laboratory—no matter what the transfer order may be. A break in the chain can prejudice a victim's case, so at each exchange point, items should be receipted.

Ideally, the prosecutor's office advises the hospital authorities on custody requirements, and appropriate systems are worked out between hospital and police department. Where no established protocol exists, a physician's direct transmission of evidence to the police probably constitutes the surest custody.

Other options: A West Coast institution's security office hand-delivers slides and other evidence from the examining physician to the laboratory. The material is analyzed and kept in the security department.

In a Texas hospital emergency room, evidence is turned over immediately to a designated laboratory official. If he is unavailable, the evidence is placed in a locked box, and only the forensic pathologist and emergency-room charge nurse have keys for it. The box is later taken by a lab representative after he signs a receipt.

CHAPTER 7

Venereal disease

Most rape victims do not contract venereal disease as a result of the rape, according to statistics. But the worry is always there, and victims should be assured that you (or institutions such as Planned Parenthood clinics or public health centers) will provide prevention or treatment.

1. Briefly describe venereal disease symptoms:
   — Syphilis produces a skin lesion or eruption (a "sore") usually on or near the genitals, rectum or mouth, though sometimes on other parts of the body, from nine to 90 days after sexual contact. Occasionally the sore is hidden from view and also unnoticed because it is painless.
   — Gonorrhea seldom produces symptoms in women, but a few may experience vaginal discharge or painful urination a few days or weeks after sexual contact.

2. Some clinics automatically screen for VDRL (Venereal Disease Research Laboratories) and GC (Gonococcus) cultures. Others, however, offer VD prophylaxis, emphasizing that the victim can choose treatment or nontreatment. (Many clinicians warn against routine antibiotic administration, but others recommend it if there's doubt about the victim's return for follow-up checks.)

3. Explain possible treatments and their side effects. The most common side effects are vaginal discharge or itching, and pain at the injection site.

25

4. If penicillin is administered:
   — Advise the victim to avoid alcoholic beverages for 48 hours after receiving penicillin treatment so that the effectiveness of the medication will not be reduced.
   — To monitor a possible allergic reaction, ask the victim to wait 30 to 45 minutes on the premises. That's her medical—and your legal—protection against anaphylactic shock. If she will not stay, describe the possible reactions: rash, swelling or itching around eyes, face, throat, ankles, stomach or behind knees. If any of these occur, she must return immediately for treatment with an antihistamine.

5. Impress each victim with the need for VDRL and GC cultures in from two to six weeks. The tests are necessary because antibiotics are not always effective (and penicillin is not effective for *prior* syphilis); the tests are absolutely essential if antibiotic treatment was refused or if spectinomycin was given.

6. VDRL and GC tests done initially will disclose presence of venereal disease prior to assault. Be aware that this information, if noted, can damage the victim's case.

Anti-VD choices

For adults

1. One gm. probenecid orally, followed by penicillin G procaine suspension 4.8 million units in two sites intramuscularly. There is no need to wait between administration of probenecid and penicil-

lin. The dose is considered effective against gonorrhea and incubating syphilis.

2. Penicillin G procaine suspension 2.4 million units intramuscularly, repeated in three days for gonorrhea; and benzathine penicillin 2.4 million units intramuscularly for syphilis.
3. Ampicillin 500 mg. orally, taken four times daily for four days.
4. Ampicillin 3.5 gm. with probenecid 1 gm. orally, taken simultaneously.
5. For penicillin-allergic victims:
   — Tetracycline HCl 1.5 gm. orally immediately and 500 mg. four times a day for 15 days; or
   — Erythromycin 500 mg. orally four times a day for 15 days; or
   — 2 gm. spectinomycin intramuscularly as a single dose. This drug is gonorrhea-specific and not effective against incubating syphilis.
6. If the victim is pregnant, the drug of choice is penicillin. If she is allergic to it, erythromycin 1.5 gm. intramuscularly at once, then 500 mg. orally four times a day for four days may be used. However, erythromycin does not cross the placenta in a dosage high enough to protect the fetus from syphilis. Tetracycline does, but can also cause stained teeth in the fetus. When this and the rareness of rape-induced syphilis are explained to the victim, she may elect later serology and treatment. Spectinomycin should be avoided because its effects in pregnant women are unknown.

For children

1. Children over 100 lbs. require adult doses.
2. Children who weigh less than 100 lbs. should receive penicillin G procaine suspension 100,000 units/kg. body weight intramuscularly, with 25 mg./kg. body weight probenecid in divided doses, at the same time.

3. Children six years or older can take oral tetracycline HCl 25 mg./kg. body weight immediately, then 40-60 mg./kg. body weight in four divided doses for seven days.
4. Children younger than six can take oral erythromycin 40 mg./kg. body weight daily in four divided doses for seven days.
5. Children not yet six years old should not be given tetracycline.
6. Recheck all dosages in PDR. Keep on hand *updated* recommendations from the CDC (Center for Disease Control, Atlanta).

CHAPTER 8

Pregnancy

Pregnancy is often the major fear of a rape victim. If antipregnancy treatment is not available through you or your institution, be prepared to name places that offer it. In all cases, after discussion of pregnancy possibility and treatment, the victim has the right to decide if she wishes treatment, and what kind. But a thorough medical history and the following counsel are necessary parts of initial physician-victim contact:

1. Pregnancy virtually can be ruled out if the victim takes the pill on the regular, prescribed basis, or wears an IUD. It can be ruled out if the victim has had a hysterectomy or tubal ligation.

2. The victim is at greatest risk from unprotected sexual intercourse during her "middle week," which includes the two or three days before the midcycle, the midcycle itself and the two or three days after.

3. If prior conception has occurred, the victim is not in danger of rape-induced pregnancy.

4. If prior conception is suspected, a pregnancy test (a new one is available that detects pregnancy four to five days after fertilization) should be performed. The test is essential if administration of DES is contemplated.

5. Victims accepting medication should return for another pregnancy test if menstruation does not occur on time.

6. Victims refusing medication also should return for a pregnancy test if menstruation does not occur on time. Delay may be caused by emotional stress. Menstrual extraction may be appropriate for and acceptable to such victims. They may elect other procedures if test results are positive. Some clinics keep signed records of victims' initial refusals of medication.

Pregnancy

Antipregnancy Rx choices

1. Diethylstilbestrol or DES (by Lilly) 25 mg. or 50 mg. in divided doses for five days. The drug has risks and side effects that the physician must carefully explain to the patient before she agrees to take it. Known as the morning-after pill (though in fact several pills make up the dose), DES is effective only if given within 72 hours after sexual assault. It is contraindicated if a prior pregnancy exists. Almost all women taking DES will experience nausea and vomiting; many also suffer headaches, irregular menses and breast tenderness. Nausea is the most troublesome side effect. It can be prevented or minimized by taking DES on a full stomach and/or by use of an antiemetic such as trimethobenzamide HCl (Tigan by Beecham) or prochlorperazine (Compazine by Smith Kline & French). The latter is more commonly administered. Ten mg. of it is given orally 30 minutes before the first DES dose, and 50 mg. taken daily for the other five days of DES medication. Extra DES should be provided to compensate for what is lost in vomiting.

DES came under attack some time ago because it can be a dangerous drug for patients with a history of or tendency to breast, uterine or cervi-

30

cal cancer; diabetes; or hypertension. In addition, undetected breast, cervical or vaginal cancers may grow if DES is administered. It also has been known to cause genital malignancies in some male and female children of women who took the drug to prevent spontaneous abortion. The risks can be decreased if the physician takes a complete, accurate medical history and performs a thorough physical exam before prescribing DES. That the drug is not to be used as a birth-control method should also be made clear to the victim.

2. Conjugated estrogens (Premarin by Ayerst) 2.5 mg. orally, four or five times a day for five days; or 25 mg. intravenously daily for three days.

3. Ethinyl estradiol (Estinyl by Schering) 0.5 mg. two times a day for four or five days.

4. Medroxyprogesterone acetate (Provera by Upjohn) 10 mg. two times a day for four days, begun within 72 hours of assault, if the rape occurred after the 18th day from the start of the menstrual cycle.

5. Abortion if medication is refused and the victim later discovers that she is pregnant. Abortion can be an emotion-laden issue for some people. It should be discussed tactfully as an option that is open to the victim.

6. Menstrual extraction procedure for victims who refused medication and fail to menstruate on time. The procedure brings on the period if the patient is not pregnant, or aborts an early pregnancy.

CHAPTER 9

Exit procedures

When the physical examination is over, the rape victim may need time to wind down, deal with her personal needs or consult a crisis counselor.

1. Give her an opportunity to wash. If she did not wash before the exam, she'll want to as soon as possible afterward.
2. Provide a wash-up area with privacy. Curtain one off if separate facilities are unavailable.
3. Supply a mouthwash for the victim who was forced into oral sexual contact.
4. Don't leave the victim alone during her clean-up, unless she specifically requests privacy; stay at least in voice contact with her.
5. If she has no clothes to substitute for those retained for evidence, arrange with family, friends or hospital to provide suitable covering for her.
6. Determine where she will go after leaving the hospital. If she was raped at home, she may prefer not to return there. Make sure that there is somewhere she can stay and feel safe.
7. Consider overnight hospital admission if the victim has severe emotional difficulties and no suitable accommodations for the next 24-48 hours.
8. Help arrange transportation. The victim will have no money if she was robbed as well as raped, and she may have come to the emergency room without friends or family. See if the hospital or nearby

crisis center will assume transportation costs. (To cover that expense, an Ohio hospital has county funds at its disposal.)

9. Discuss the physical symptoms she may notice in the days or weeks to come. Also give her written instructions concerning her medications and their side effects. Don't assume that she'll absorb your oral instructions; patients under stress seldom do.

10. Give her a phone number to call if she has any questions or if any alarming symptoms appear after leaving the premises.

11. Provide the names, addresses and phone numbers of local organizations that give psychological/psychiatric/crisis counseling, VD and pregnancy tests or abortion services. Planned Parenthood clinics, YWCAs, municipal health agencies, and crisis groups (or private physicians and therapists) are the usual community sources. If the state has a crime compensation board, tell the victim about it.

12. Arrange for follow-up care:
   — Make a definite two-week appointment (or two- and six-week appointments), stating date, time and clinic location.
   — Advise her to have a pregnancy test (the first or the second) within two weeks after a missed menstrual period.
   — Explain menstrual extraction.
   — Remind her to return for removal of stitches, if she has had them.
   — Advise her to return for evaluation of wound-healing even if she was given tetanus toxoid.

CHAPTER 10

Police role

In most rape cases, there are no witnesses. The victim is the single source of immediate information, and dealing with her is a delicate process. She must be convinced of the police officer's genuine concern while being asked probing, disturbing questions. Moreover, she should be subjected to only one in-depth interview. To achieve maximum results in minimum time and with least additional trauma to the victim, police department leaders must first inquire into local emergency-room rape-case procedures. Where necessary, these procedures—specifically, the interview facilities, laboratory facilities and chain of evidence-custody system—should be cooperatively improved. Thereafter:

1. Give rape cases priority. If possible, assign a special force or, in smaller departments, one detective to respond immediately to a rape call-in. (Some cities have sex-crime units composed of well-trained male and female members on 24-hour call.) Have interpreters available, in case the victim speaks no English.

2. If the suspect is apprehended quickly at or near the scene of the crime, make sure the victim, for her safety, is not seen as she identifies him.

3. Interview the victim in the most comfortable surroundings possible—her home, if the rape did not occur there, or a private hospital area set aside for that purpose. Do not insist on an immediate station house interview if other facilities are unavail-

able. Wait until the next day. The victim may have given a preliminary statement to a police officer and then left for medical care. In either case, she may be too physically or emotionally exhausted to cooperate.

4. Allow no more than two police officers to be present no matter where the interview is conducted. Exclude family and friends. However, if it will comfort the victim and facilitate the interview, allow the presence of a neutral support person (female nurse or counselor).

5. Establish rapport with the victim by words and attitude:
    — Courteously introduce yourself without appearing stiff and formal.
    — Explain why the interview is necessary.
    — Choose careful language; for example, never refer to any sex act as "perverted."
    — Avoid any suggestion of force in your questions and your manner of asking them. It will distress the victim and remind her of force used during the rape.

6. Determine whether the victim was acquainted with the assailant. Use questions such as: How long did you know him? How did you meet? How would you describe your relationship?

7. Avoid questions that elicit a yes/no response. Instead, aim for open-ended queries such as: Tell me more about . . . What happened after . . . ? that invite descriptive answers.

8. Maintain a patient, gentle attitude. The victim's embarrassment and shame are aggravated by discussing the traumatic experience (which she'd like to forget) with a stranger. Telling the story can be so frightening that some victims' psychological defenses interfere with their recall of the details of

the rape, according to one police training manual.

9. While being firm that the interview *must* continue, offer the victim small human comforts—sympathy for her ordeal; a chance to express her feelings or to cry; a rest period for coffee; a cigarette; or a visit to the washroom.

10. Go over the affidavit with her. Is it accurate? Complete? Would she suggest changes? Now is the time to make them.

11. Explain what further legal procedures will take place if she goes through with prosecution and the case goes to court.

12. Be tactful with family members. They, too, according to a *Police Chief* article, are in a crisis state and need assurance that they and the victim are guilty of no wrongdoing. Assure them that the victim acted correctly; otherwise she might not be alive. Include family in the investigative—but not the interview—process. Ask for information that may help apprehend the assailant.

For children

Only after parents are made aware that their behavior can affect the child (make her feel guilty or more frightened) should an interview with the child take place, according to some authorities. Specialists act as on-call interviewers of very young victims in other countries, but the United States has no established system. However, a few guidelines have been developed:

1. In advance, determine from others the child's level of psychosexual development and understanding of the occurrences.

2. As with adults, conduct the interview in privacy, but permit the presence of another person as an

observer—preferably someone not emotionally involved in the incident.

3. Create a friendly, nonthreatening atmosphere by asking the child general questions: Where do you live? What are the names of your close relatives? Favorite friends? Favorite TV shows? Hobbies? What do you like about school? Do you know what "telling the truth" means?

Police role

4. After establishing the child's level of maturity and concepts of truthfulness, ask what took place between her and the assailant. Use vocabulary the child will understand.

5. Allow the child to describe the event in her own way. Do not ask leading questions or put words in the child's mouth. To simplify explanations, she can point to parts of the body involved, or draw a picture of what happened.

6. If the case is to be brought to court, explain court procedures to the parents. Ideally, they prepare the child for that experience.

CHAPTER 11

Criminal justice/ prosecutor's office

For centuries, criminal justice was out of balance for rape victims, their plight being overshadowed by ''rights of the defendant.'' Recently, however, the inequity has been recognized, some laws changed and the manner in which prosecutors relate to victims improved. (Ideally, a single prosecutor handles a case from complaint through trial.) To help achieve these goals within your own community, the following steps are recommended to prosecutors' offices:

For institutions

1. Meet with hospital, laboratory and police staffs to discuss evidentiary needs and evidence custody.
2. Jointly establish a rape procedures protocol that protects the victim, and a formal policy that interlocks responsibilities.
3. Streamline the roles that hospital or private physicians must play in their court appearances. Work out an on-call system for court appearances.
4. Assure medical personnel they are required to attest only to observations recorded during the medical examination. They will *not* be asked for opinions as to whether victims were raped. Understanding this may decrease physicians' resistance to court appearances.
5. To encourage cooperation, offer to meet with the physician to discuss details about the case.

39

6. Keep all medical, police and laboratory personnel who have been involved in the case informed about its progress and outcome. Small courtesies foster and help maintain cooperativeness.

For the victim

1. Be patient yet thorough. Remember that the victim may have told the story many times over and may now be inclined to skirt the facts. You need them all. But be sure to gain her confidence at the initial meeting; you can get detailed information about the incident later.
2. Describe the options and problems of the criminal-justice system. Advance explanations help eliminate pretrial anxiety. Assure her you will thoroughly prepare her for the trial.
3. Establish easy two-way ongoing communication: Give her your phone number and extension, and have her provide the phone numbers of her residence, place of employment and of friends with whom she may stay. Discuss how you should identify yourself to minimize embarrassment when you call her.
4. Determine if the victim plans to leave the area temporarily or permanently, and how she can be reached if and when her presence is needed.
5. Advise her that she is not obliged to give information to the defendant, his lawyer, family or friends. If they harass her, she may report that to the police.
6. Tell the victim at what point in the proceedings she may have to face the defendant. Advance warning may decrease her distress.
7. Discuss typical defense-attorney questions so that

the victim will be prepared to answer them.

8. Make her aware of tricky word-phrasing common-ly used in court. For example, in trying to suggest mistaken identity, the defense attorney may ask: "Did the man who raped you have a mustache?" (rather than "Did my client have a mustache?"). If the victim answers yes and the defendant is now clean-shaven, there will be doubts about her memory or veracity. She's on surer ground if she points to the defendant and says, "He had a mustache at the time," or something similar.

9. Remember that witnesses' rights and obligations are important to the victim and others called to the stand. The following guidelines will help them:
   — Listen to the question carefully. If you do not understand it, say so.
   — If you don't know the answer, say so.
   — If you can't recall the answer, say so.
   — If you know the answer to a question, give it concisely, but supply just the information requested—nothing more.
   — Never try to explain or qualify an answer with words such as "Yes, but . . ."

10. If necessary, help the victim arrange for transportation to and from court, and for getting time off from her job.

11. Suggest that the victim bring a supportive friend or family member to court on the trial day. If none is available, arrange for a rape-crisis center counselor to accompany the victim.

12. When appropriate, offer sources for psychological or psychiatric counseling. The need for it may become acute as the trial date approaches and the victim must relive her experience.

Criminal justice/ prosecutor's office

For the child victim

1. Treat the child gently at all times.
2. Provide a specially trained interviewer, if possible. In one city, neither police department nor prosecutor's office members are permitted to interview a child victim. She is interviewed by a third party, a member of a police youth division.
3. Keep in mind always that not only the interview but the court appearance also may be traumatic to the child. She should be shielded from it, according to some psychiatrists. This is the law in some countries but is not yet a workable solution here.
4. Prepare the child for the trial, after establishing her level of understanding. Role-playing techniques or a mock trial are helpful.
5. Arrange to have the court closed to the public, if possible.
6. Keep parents or guardians advised as to procedures and progress.

Are rapists sexually impaired?

Conviction of rapists is often difficult, especially if no sperm is found on or within the victim's body. But perhaps the case should not hinge alone on that particular evidence, or lack of it.

Recent research establishes that some rapists suffer a sexual dysfunction. Specifically, an assailant may have been unable to ejaculate normally, say Dr. A. Nicholas Groth and Dr. Ann Wolbert Burgess, who conducted a study of 170 inmates at the Massachusetts Center for Diagnosis and Treatment of Sexually Dangerous Persons.

Through clinical and personal interviews, the doctors discovered a high rate of abnormalities such as premature, delayed and failed ejaculation (even degrees of impotence) among study participants. More than a third of them admitted to sexual dysfunction during the assault, a condition that they did not experience during their nonassaultive, consenting sexual relations. Fifteen per cent of these men had retarded ejaculation. That, the doctors claim, is markedly different from the incidence noted in the general population: one in 700 men.

Drs. Groth and Burgess then did a study of 129 rape victims treated at the Boston City Hospital emergency room. No sperm was found in more than half these victims, though some said they had been raped by more than one man. This supports the earlier findings.

The researchers' report appeared in the October 6, 1977, issue of *The New England Journal of Medicine.* An accompanying editorial added: "Since we do not have information about the rapists who are not apprehended and convicted, we do not know if they are a different population with different motivations and symptoms."

Criminal justice/ prosecutor's office

CHAPTER 12

Crisis intervention

If medical and police/legal personnel care properly for rape victims, are crisis-intervention counselors necessary? Yes. Rape is a life-threatening, violent experience. As a result, victims are in a state of crisis and require special emotional support and guidance. Who can provide crisis intervention? Hospital social workers. Psychiatric, emergency-room or OB/gyn nurses. Pastoral counselors. Medical students. Crisis-center workers. Visiting nurses. Special-unit police officers. All must be specially trained to give immediate, short-term support to the rape victim and see that her physical, medical and psychological needs are met. (Few, however, should be expected to manage the long-term counseling required by unusually traumatized victims or those with prior emotional difficulties. They generally require psychiatrists, psychologists or psychiatric social workers.)

Rape programs that include round-the-clock seven-days-a-week counseling service have been established at some hospitals. One in Ohio, for example, immediately and routinely phones an on-call volunteer at the city's rape-crisis center when a victim arrives at the emergency room and has consented to this intervention. An Illinois hospital uses trained chaplains, a group with a large number of males—all instructed in follow-up counseling as well. A New York City hospital uses female medical students as support persons and medical-care coordinators.

Wherever the counselor comes from, he or she must be able to project both compassion and objectivity. The counselor needs information from the victim, and the victim needs information and sympathy from the counselor. Here's how to make the most of this two-way process:

1. Focus on the victim's emotional and physical state (she may be exhausted from stress and lack of sleep over the past 12 or 24 hours), and on how she expresses her feelings. She will provide verbal and nonverbal clues to her needs and how you can fill them. Try to accommodate hospital procedures to her needs.

2. Encourage the victim to talk about the experience, after assuring her that you understand the factors inhibiting her from facing and sharing the trauma. Allow her outward expressions of anger (which may be directed at you and others involved) because anger turned inward can be detrimental.

3. Relieve her anxiety with reassurance about, for example, the medical examination, how her family may respond to the occurrence and what other victims have felt. Encourage the victim to make decisions. In that way, she'll regain the control of her life that was lost during the rape.

4. Anticipate a variety of emotions. Fear is the most common emotion felt during the rape ("I thought I was going to die") and, for some victims, after, especially if the assailant threatened retaliation for her reporting the crime. Shame and shock are almost universal feelings. Others are guilt, disbelief, humiliation, embarrassment, helplessness and defilement.

5. Anticipate a variety of physical reactions. Some victims fidget, cry, shake, chain-smoke, laugh, rock, chatter, stare—or swing from one phase to another, all of them normal "expressed reactions." Other victims may appear calm and composed—the "controlled reaction"—which may be

their habitual way of dealing with stress. It does not mean they are unaffected by the experience. Indeed, they need crisis intervention as much as distraught victims.

6. Discuss forms she will be asked to sign that contain consent to general and gynecological examinations, release of information and the taking of photographs. Explain that the forms ensure victim privacy and limit hospital rights to release patient information.

7. Be sure she understands what she is signing. (In bilingual communities, an interpreter should be available or the reverse side of the form can be printed in the appropriate language.)

8. If an adult victim or parents of a minor will not sign forms, record the fact.

9. Follow established institution policy concerning minors who request information but do not want parents or guardians to be informed.

10. Suggest to the victim (but do not coerce her) that she report the crime to the police. Explain police procedures and how her reporting helps police to construct the rapist's modus operandi. For example, many rapists have a compulsive once-or-

Hotline for men

Fathers, husbands or boyfriends may express a desire to "get the guy and kill him." Persuade them that such action can only add to the problem. These men need help in dealing with their violent reactions, and in relating thereafter to the victim herself. A Missouri hospital has a volunteer system in which husbands of victims talk with other husbands or boyfriends of victims.

twice-a-week pattern. Knowing the pattern can aid police in apprehending the rapist and saving another female from rape. But remind her that the decision is hers and that medical treatment will not be withheld if she refuses. (In some cases, the victim's chances of quick recovery are improved without the legal burden.) A few jurisdictions allow third-party reporting by a crisis counselor or physician who gives crime details but not the victim's name. Act appropriately after checking state laws concerning reporting of child abuse.

11. Help family members and friends by letting them ventilate their feelings *away from* the victim, but urge them to allow the victim to talk about the assault, even though it may be difficult for them to listen to the details. Help them channel their distress and anger properly: toward prosecution. In all cases, but especially in child assault, emphasize that the first concern should be for the victim's physical and emotional welfare.

12. Consult other chapters in this manual for assorted steps that can be taken by a crisis-intervention counselor in place of—or in addition to—the procedures that medical/legal personnel follow.

Short-term follow-up

Burgess and Holmstrom conclude from their extensive work that victims fall into patterns, the rape-trauma syndrome. Sutherland and Scherl (see bibliography in the Appendix) find that, during days and weeks after rape, the victim moves toward decreased anxiety and willingness to deal with the consequences of the event. No rigid rules apply, since each victim is unique. Here's what to look for:

1. The acute phase may cause complete disruption of

life style or psychiatric disturbances requiring immediate psychiatric/psychological help.

2. Some victims exhibit muscular tension, insomnia, loss of appetite or difficulty in eating, urinary or vaginal discomfort, general nervousness and irritability—or any combination of these.

3. In the second phase, some victims begin reorganizing their lives. They may decide to move, take a trip or they may turn to family and friends for resumption of normal living.

4. At this phase, some victims begin to suppress memories of, or altogether to deny, the event.

5. The second phase may also include persisting physical reactions: nightmares, phobias about going out at night or to places reminiscent of the rape scene, fear of men, aversion to sex.

6. In the final phase, depression may set in. Many victims feel the need to talk more than before. They should be assured that counseling and other treatment are always available to them.

For child victims

1. Very young children may seem unconcerned about the event before and after the medical/legal aspects have been attended to. Parents should be advised to monitor the child's behavior (sometimes for years) and deal with reactions openly and supportively.

2. Many youngsters manifest reactions nonverbally through loss of appetite, unwillingness to go to school, difficulty with school work, sleeping problems or nightmares and sometimes vomiting.

3. Young victims may develop distorted body and sexual images.

4. Teen-age victims often "feel different" from their peers, and this can be traumatic.
5. If the victim was a virgin, there may be problems in establishing a future sexual relationship.
6. If a court appearance is necessary, the child's anxieties may be increased and the after-rape symptoms exacerbated.

Crisis intervention

CHAPTER 13

Counseling of family and friends

by Theresa L. Crenshaw, M.D.

Family structure can fall apart in the aftermath of sexual assault, whether it involves an adult or a child. Reports say that from 50 to 80 per cent of raped women lose their boyfriends or husbands as a consequence of the sexual assault. There are no reliable statistics on the separation of parents following sexual molestation of their child. Yet, clinical evidence suggests that sexual assault of a child can spell the end of a marital relationship having other serious problems, or can precipitate stresses even a good marriage may not survive.

Therapy for the victim alone is seldom sufficient to prevent severe relationship difficulties. Family members and "significant others" in her life must be willing to accept advice or treatment themselves for the rape victim's and the relationship's total recovery.

The adult victim

If the relationships that a victim has with the "significant others" in her life are secure and fundamentally sound, the rape-trauma syndrome will be less intense. But the woman who loses her external support system following rape may fall apart altogether because the sexual assault has also temporarily disrupted her internal support system.

The *external support system* includes those persons or things in the environment that an individual needs for security and stability: husband, family, friends, home, religion, work, police, doctors, lawyers, society. The *internal support system* consists of an individual's physical and mental health, which enable that person to cope or to progress even in the absence of a functional external support system.

A disruption of either system constitutes a crisis.

Additionally, as a result of the sexual assault, the woman may develop sexual aversion—the most threatening consequence to her bond with husband or lover. Unrecognized, undiagnosed and untreated, sexual aversion is often the main reason why such relationships wither and die.

It is not surprising that the rape victim's behavior often puzzles family and friends. While they may be very supportive initially, after several months their patience is gone. The rape victim is reacting out of proportion to the crisis, they believe. Proper counsel in advance will prepare them to deal with problems as they occur, and encourage them to seek additional therapeutic help if it is needed.

Preventative counseling

1. Explain the rape-trauma syndrome and how to minimize it as soon as possible after the assault—at a time that is medically and psychologically appropriate.
2. Eliminate the issue of victim guilt or responsibility by emphasizing the rapist's *crime*.
3. Eliminate the issue of a partner's guilt feelings. Assure him that he could not have anticipated or prevented the rape.
4. Discourage his angry, destructive or irrational attempts to find the rapist.
5. Suggest that he discuss their sexual relationship with her, convincing her that his feelings haven't changed (if that is the case) and that he still desires her sexually. He can also tell her that he will wait until she initiates sex, that she can approach him

Counseling of family and friends

52

when she feels comfortable again. If a month passes without return to their normal sexual relations, short-term sex therapy is indicated.

6. Explain that the earlier crisis-intervention therapy is initiated, the less is needed. Three to six hours is usually enough if therapy begins within one or two weeks of the assault.

7. Discuss venereal disease and pregnancy. Ensure that both victim and partner are aware of the possible consequences of rape, know the appropriate precautions to take and are informed of treatment options.

Therapeutic intervention

1. If the partner feels sexually different toward the victim, help him to identify components of the change and to see their incongruity.

2. If sexual aversion develops in the victim, short-term sexual therapy is indicated for both the victim and her partner.

3. If the partner is reacting in a destructive, angry, irrational manner, redirect his energy toward being supportive and useful to the victim.

4. Men differ in their ability to accept and cope with the partner's rape experience. Much depends on many variables: age, religion, upbringing, duration of the relationship, severity of physical and psychological trauma for the female, degree of ego and machismo involved. Identify the variables and put them in proper perspective. The male may not be aware he is having difficulty or needs help, but a perceptive counselor can observe the male, through the woman's eyes, and call him into therapy when it appears necessary.

In summary, family and friends are often too tangled in

**Counseling
of family
and friends**

their own emotional responses to be of much assistance to the rape victim. Legal procedures sometimes replace thoughtful medical care. Our police methods and legal system often add to the trauma by trying the victim and acquitting the rapist.

While attitudes and social systems are improving, many rape victims are caught in the transition. In the meantime, appropriate counseling of the victim and her "significant others" can help minimize the rape-trauma syndrome.

The child victim

In my professional experience, approximately 80 per cent of children who are molested or raped never tell anyone, not even their parents. About 90 per cent of child molestation known to the parents is unreported to the authorities. But the family dynamics precipitated by child molestation are distinct from those precipitated by assault of an adult. Young boys as well as young girls can, of course, be victims of molestation. I will follow the author's example, and refer to the victim as "she."

No matter how well it is handled, almost every instance of child molestation results in some short-term observable consequences in the child's behavior and adjustment and in the parent relationship. These depend on two major variables. One is the nature of the assault itself.

When the child has had her underpants pulled down or been fondled without penetration or injury, and has not been frightened, the incident can be relatively problem-free. But if the child has been raped and if physical injury has occurred, the psychological resources of the parents are more severely pressed.

The closeness of the assailant to the family is the second variable. It is a matter of degree: Effects will likely be more severe if he is the father rather than the stepfather or mother's boyfriend; more severe if he is an older brother rather than a grandfather or a cousin; more severe if he is a family friend rather than a stranger.

Clearly, therapy for the child is usually accomplished by treating and educating the parents as well, especially when the child is very young.

Exploring parental reaction patterns, as perceived by the child, will be valuable to the counselor:

The parents do not believe the child. If the child is not believed, she faces a psychological issue that has little specific relationship to the assault's sexual nature. It may be the first time this child has turned to the parents in any crisis or serious need. The message "I don't believe you" is translated by the child as "I won't help you." The child's security and support system is altered in a way the child cannot comprehend. Once confident that any broken toy can be repaired and that any injury will mend with a kiss, young children learn gradually that there are things even their parents cannot fix. Children integrate these experiences into their maturing process. However, they are unable to integrate a parental message that says, "I will not help." Most children who have had this experience report a sense of betrayal and desertion that continues thereafter to affect the fundamental bond between parent and child.

In fact, this child has been psychologically abandoned long before she is able to be self-sufficient. As a consequence, severe anxieties and neuroses often develop and are difficult to treat without the parents' full cooperation. Generally, they are unaware of the child's sense of psychological desertion, and are merely protecting themselves from truths too difficult to handle. Skillful counseling enables them to understand the child's needs and face the situation.

The parents believe the child but are unable to acknowledge or deal with the incident directly. The child who is believed by her parents but told to keep the incident a secret is better off. She may feel confused about the experience and feel she has done something wrong, something too terrible to be discussed. However, she does not experience a sense of betrayal and abandonment. The relationship between parents and child is not greatly altered unless the parents become overprotective out of guilt and concern.

The parents become extremely upset and react in an irrational manner. In this instance, the child is believed, and some type of dramatic action ensues. The parents take the child to the doctor or the emergency room and demand a pelvic examination, even though the child may state she was not touched. The parents behave as though the child has been damaged or dirtied, and may actually verbalize such thoughts in the child's presence. She may grow up with the misconception that somehow she is genitally abnormal, or deformed by the experience. The angry father may threaten to find and kill the assailant. The child may be embarrassed at school if the incident becomes public knowledge. The parents frequently scold the child for having allowed the incident to occur. In addition, whether three years old or a teen-ager, the child may even be accused of being seductive or promiscuous.

The parents believe the child, discuss the incident with the child, reassure her and take appropriate measures to prevent a recurrence of the incident. This is, of course, the best but, unfortunately, the most uncommon response. When it occurs, therapy is rarely required.

In the first three instances, these conflicts can result:

1. If the parents are already having relationship difficulties, they may be increased by the sexual assault and early reactions of husband and wife. Old grievances may surface while each blames the other in some way for not taking measures to prevent the assault.

2. Uncertainty over how to handle the incident may cause disagreements, which may be open and angry or quiet and passive. The profound anxiety and concern of the parents may be the cause of

discord that ends with resentment and blame.

3. Discipline of the child, with the intention of preventing future similar incidents, may cause additional discord.

4. Family life style may undergo a radical change (which may be traumatic in itself), such as having grandmother move in to baby-sit, or moving to a different town to avoid the scandal.

5. Family relationships can change in direct proportion to the closeness of the relatives. Family members who believe the child may align themselves against family members who don't. If the child is living with a divorced parent, the molestation may precipitate a custody battle.

6. Mothers may develop generalized suspicion and distrust of males, including the father or stepfather, especially if the molester was someone she once trusted.

7. The child's behavior may change in mild or severe manner. She may go through periods of thumb-sucking, nightmares, emotional withdrawal, poor school performance, rebelliousness or obvious attention-getting attempts to sustain the level of adult interest incurred by the molestation.

8. Finally, parents tend to blame the molestation for any of the child's subsequent undesirable behavior. They become unduly concerned about what are perhaps normal or common developmental phases, easily explained by a professional.

Until these conflicts are resolved, the parents will be unable to help their child. The following steps are valuable:

1. When parents first speak to emergency-room personnel or a counselor, they may express doubts about the child's truthfulness. Encourage them to believe the child, unless her claims are *proven* untrue. Trust is essential for the long-term rela-

Counseling of family and friends

tionship of parent and child. The other side of the coin is that few children trust their parents enough to feel comfortable telling them about this kind of experience. When the child does tell, the parents must not jeopardize that trust. Actually, children seldom lie about such experiences, and most youngsters, despite their tender years, are able to distinguish between fact and fancy.

2. The physician or counselor can ask one or both parents to witness the examination and treatment if the parental attitude is not destructive to the child or critical of the procedures. As a rule, the child is reassured by the mother's or father's presence. Parents who cannot bear to observe such procedures will need to hear—from physician or counselor—what was done and how conclusions were drawn. For example: "The doctor examined the external genitals. They appeared normal with no lacerations or bruises. An attempt to introduce a small finger into the opening of the vagina was not possible, indicating that the hymen and vagina are unharmed. There is no evidence of bleeding and no reason to be concerned about any injury to the genital area or other parts of the body."

   If an injury has occurred, regardless of how minor, the physician or counselor can diagram or describe it for the parents in simple terms. Do not assume the parents know anything about physiology and anatomy. Explain them thoroughly in layman's language.

3. Parents will need help identifying and successfully dealing with guilt they feel as a result of the incident. Point out that conscientious monitoring of the child 24 hours a day would be unrealistic and ultimately harmful.

4. 'Parents need to know how to cope with the child's

reactions, and when they must simply let time take its course. Short-term and long-term consequences of the assault should be discussed, as well as its effects on their child's future psychosexual development. Reassure parents that the experience, handled appropriately, need leave no emotional scars.

5. Information about normal developmental sexuality in children benefits parents. They tend to perceive any sexual behavior that follows the assault as an outgrowth of the experience, and thereafter often scrutinize a child's sexuality. They may notice for the first time behavior that has been present all along, and react with some alarm. In addition, a three- or four-year-old may have found the genital fondling experienced during molestation so enjoyable that she continues it on her own. But discovery and stimulation of the genitals is part of growing up. It is harmless unless the parents react adversely.

6. Few parents know that young children have vaginal discharges that are natural and normal. If they are first discovered after the assault, parents have a new worry. Taking a culture of the vaginal discharge is simple and reassuring for all. However, because young girls sometimes develop urinary-tract infections following genital fondling, parents should pay attention to any complaints of burning on urination or urinary frequency. Some raped children do contract venereal disease, and routine culturing of the vaginal canal (and the ejaculate of the rapist, if possible) is desirable. When VD occurs, it's frequently missed because it's unsuspected.

"Who are child molesters' likely targets?" professionals are sometimes asked. Youngsters who are timid, afraid,

Counseling of family and friends

neurotic, whining, unable to relate comfortably to anyone but perhaps mother and father are rarely molested. These children will not cuddle in a lap, or express warmth or affection. They are by nature distrustful and anxious. The outgoing, curious, explorative, tender, affectionate and happy young child is the more usual target for sexual assaults. It is outrageous that some attorneys or other professionals refer to these young children as promiscuous. It is disturbing to consider also the number of articles implying or stating that incest was the result of a frigid wife and a seductive child. Yet I know of no article that deals with the central issue of any child molestation: a person with poor judgment and inadequate impulse control.

The sexual-trauma syndrome experienced by the child can be relatively innocuous if the parents handle it well and no physical injury occurred. Parents never intend to react in a way that is destructive to the child. Most simply need some therapeutic guidance from a properly trained counselor, particularly in recognizing early symptoms of trauma. A single or obvious solution seldom exists. However, with the assistance of a counselor, parents can make the appropriate legal and family decisions, and prevent many—if not all—sexual-trauma syndrome consequences.

CHAPTER 14

Continuity of victim care

Growing interest in victimology has lately improved rape-victim care. Women's groups have been active in bringing rape issues to the attention of policymakers. Concerned citizens within communities have applied pressures on behalf of victims (and should continue to do so). Increasingly, formal care policies are being adopted. They work well, however, only with maximum cooperation among and within all involved agencies.

One problem common to all relates to *continuity* of victim treatment. Are care-providers able to guarantee it? Not in most instances. Agency 1 may act vigorously on the victim's behalf, while Agency 2 can render only token service. The emergency room doesn't know if the victim kept appointments made for her. Assignment of different investigators at various stages of the case destroys the rapport established initially, weakens the victim's trust in the system and influences her to drop the charges. The structure collapses without support from all sides. Some of these weaknesses stem from political considerations, budget and staffing problems, lack of administration's interest and internal power struggles. However, they can be overcome:

The Hennepin County Sexual Assault Service in Minneapolis eliminated the difficulties by coordinating efforts of police, physicians, social workers and the criminal-justice system under a Law Enforcement Assistance Agency (LEAA) grant. The system is unusual because it can be directed by a part-time prosecutor working within a small community or by an attorney in a large prosecutor's office.

The Seattle Rape Reduction Project coordinates activities of Seattle police, Harborview Medical Center, the county prosecutor's office, and a YWCA crisis center. Since the project's September 1973 inception, more women than ever before have requested treatment, reported the assault and then prosecuted it.

Special training

Everyone responsible for part of the rape victims' care benefits from in-service training. It should include definition of medical/legal policies and procedures; needs and reactions of victims; and crisis-intervention techniques. Workshops or seminars with group interaction and role playing are especially helpful.

Courses can be given by crisis-center counselors, prosecutors, psychologists or police officers and nurses with experience and expertise. Members of coroner's offices and police laboratories can lecture at hospitals on specifics such as recovering blood and semen stains and foreign matter, and the time elements involved. Professional societies can devote part of their meeting time to the subject.

Though early-stage training (at medical, nursing or law schools or police academies) is probably best, it's in use in only a few places: John Jay College of Criminal Justice, New York City; Downstate Medical College School of Nursing, New York City (courses for both medical students and nurses); Iona College, New Rochelle, N.Y. (courses for police, crisis counselors and nurses); and Boston College (course for nurses).

Another issue: Are rape victims helped more by females than by males? No one can say for sure, but authorities agree that (1) if the victim requests a female professional, one should be made available, if possible; and (2) more important than the professional's sex is his or her sensitivity—an attribute found in both genders but not in all people.

Good training and inter/intra-agency cooperation are not enough to ensure humane treatment of rape victims. The *attitude* of everyone involved with her counts heavily, and many people are still convinced that the victim "asked for her trouble and should get herself out of it somehow."

This is a malignancy that must be excised.

One way is to create community education programs. Handbooks and lectures should be provided for high school students and community groups such as PTAs, service clubs and even social organizations. Qualified individuals should willingly participate in radio or TV discussions on rape, or prepare articles covering necessary changes in rape laws and how rape-victim treatment can be improved. Back to square one: If you or a loved one were raped, you'd want the best of treatment for yourself or that victim.

Perhaps the most fitting closing for this chapter is the following paper prepared by the D.C. Rape Crisis Center:

A note to those closest to rape victims: Families, lovers, and friends

How does rape affect a woman? How does rape affect those closest to a rape victim? How can those closest to a rape victim do "the right thing"? We have some ideas which we wish to share with you, and we hope they will offer a beginning for giving effective support to victims of rape. For more than anyone else, it is those closest to a victim who influence how she will deal with the attack.

Most women who have been raped do not react to the sexual aspects of the crime, but instead they react to the terror and fear that is involved. Often an immediate reaction of the woman is "I could have been killed." Many of those around her, particularly men, may find themselves concerned with the sexual aspects of the crime. The more this preoccupation is communicated to the woman the more

Continuity of victim care

63

likely she is to have difficulties in dealing with her own feelings. Probably the best way to understand her feelings is to try to remember or imagine a situation where you felt powerless and afraid. You may remember feeling very alone, fearful and needing comfort.

Often the raped woman needs much love and support the first few days. Affection seems to be important. Stroking or caressing can be comforting. They help break down the loneliness and alienation. This, of course, leads to the question of sex. It is impossible to generalize about how the woman will feel about sex, nor should you guess. If you have been involved sexually with the woman, try to discuss, at an appropriate time, how she feels in general about the attack, about you, about sex. (An appropriate time is not right after the rape. Let her comments to the first two questions guide you in deciding whether you have chosen a good time to discuss it or whether you would be pushing the point too soon.) Some women will be anxious to resume normal sexual relations as a way of forgetting the rape; others will be more hesitant.

In the case of virgin rapes, female support seems most important. It is a good time to discuss the pleasure involved in sex—as well as to reassert the woman's right to decide when and with whom she wishes to have sex. Hopefully, a woman's mother will feel comfortable about this; if not, a friend or sister—especially if she [herself] has been raped—might help.

It seems advisable for the woman to talk about the rape; however, it is not possible to generalize about how much she should be encouraged to talk about it. Women do not seem to appreciate specific questions; they tend to be too probing and callous. To probe in these areas may only worsen any problems the woman may have in dealing with the rape.

Instead, questions about how she feels now and what bothers her the most are more useful. They are not threatening and should allow her to talk about her most immediate concerns. Remember, too, the woman wants to talk about other things. Often the rape may leave a woman concentrating on other problems, and it is important that she talk about these. Probably the most practical suggestion is that you communicate your own willingness to let her talk. Because of your closeness to her, the woman may be more sensitive to your feelings. If the rape distresses you, it may be impossible for her to talk to you. She may also try to protect you. In these and other cases, where she really will not be able to talk with you—encourage her to speak with someone she trusts. Remember that the rape has brought up feelings of powerlessness—encouraging her to talk to whom she wants, when she wants is more helpful than feeling that it is necessary to talk to you.

If rape is treated as a serious crime and not a heinous experience, women would probably have fewer difficulties in dealing with it. The woman survived the attack, and one would suppose that she would want to resume living a "normal" life as quickly as possible. In a healthy, supportive environment, most women will find the rape meshes with other unhappy experiences in their lives. Because of others' reactions, or their own life situations at the time of the rape, other women will find the rape was indeed a traumatic milestone. If after a reasonable amount of time, a woman seems unable to cope with the day-to-day problems of life, professional help may be sought.

Whether or not professional counseling is sought, it is not a replacement for warm, concerned, loving communication. A professional counselor may help, but he or she cannot replace your role in the relationship. Rape not only affects the woman, but also you, as it plays upon your own fears and fantasies. Try to recognize the fears for what they are; otherwise, you may end up projecting them on the woman and cause some serious problems for her and your relationship.

Finally, it should be noted that, if the woman has pressed charges, the whole process involves numerous hassles and stresses. Your awareness of the legal processes and problems involved and your support will be helpful.

Used with permission of the D.C. Rape Crisis Center.

Continuity of victim care

Contents

This reference material offers additional insights into the crime of rape, victims' rights and how both are handled by various institutions throughout the country. Readers may find the procedure descriptions and forms particularly useful. Though not every one may be reproduced without permission of the originators, all may be adapted to your agency's needs.

Used with permission of:

Appendix contents

69

*Prepared by Center for Women Policy Studies, Washington, D.C., LEAA Grant No. 74-DF-99-006, supported by the National Institute of Law Enforcement and Criminal Justice, Law Enforcement Assistance Administration, U.S. Department of Justice.

70

RIGHTS OF RAPE VICTIMS

Every victim of sexual assault should have the right:

— to be treated with dignity and respect by institutional and legal personnel

— to be given as much credibility as a victim of any other crime

— to be considered a victim of rape when any unwanted act of sex is forced on her through any type of coercion, violent or otherwise

— to be asked only those questions that are relevant to a court case or to medical treatment

— not to report the rape to the police

— to receive medical and mental health treatment, or participate in legal procedures only after giving her informed consent

— not to be exposed to prejudice against race, age, class, life style or occupation

— not to be asked questions about prior sexual experience

— to be treated in a manner that does not usurp control from the victim, but enables her to determine her own needs and how to meet them

— to have access to support persons, such as advocates, outside of the institutions

**Rights of
rape victims**

— to receive prompt medical and mental health services, whether or not the rape is reported to the police, and at no cost

— to be protected from future assault

— to be provided with information about all possible options related to legal and medical procedures

— to have her name kept from the news media

— to be considered a victim of rape regardless of the assailant's relationship to the victim, such as the victim's spouse

— to deter her assailant by any means necessary; no woman should be criminally prosecuted for harming her assailant during or within a reasonable period of time after the rape or attempted rape

— to be provided with information about her rights

— to have access to peer counseling

— to receive medical treatment without parental consent if she is a minor

— to have the best possible collection of evidence for court

— to have legal representation

— to have a preliminary hearing in each case when an arrest has been made

— to be advised of the possibility of a civil suit

Used with permission of the Rape Crisis Center, Washington, D.C.

HOSPITAL REPORT: SUSPECTED SEXUAL ASSAULT

Name of Hospital:	Patient's I.D. No.

Instructions:
1. Request immediate consult with Dept. of OBS/GYN or other appropriate Dept.
2. If patient not with a police officer **and consents,** call police.

I IDENTIFICATION

Name of Patient	Date	Time admitted to ER a.m. p.m.	Sex	Birthdate
Address		Telephone Day: Eve:	Contact (if no phone) Name: Tel:	

II CONSENTS

1. I _____ hereby authorize Dr(s). _____ and the Medical Staff of
(print full name of patient)   (print full name/names)
_____ Hospital to perform on me a physical examination and administer routine treatment on the basis thereof.

2. I DO ☐ DO NOT ☐ authorize this hospital to supply laboratory specimens and copies of all medical reports pertinent to this visit and chief complaint to the Police Department and District Attorney's office having jurisdiction. Additionally, the consequences of releasing the aforementioned material have been fully explained to me in the language I understand.

Patient's Signature	Date
Patient or Guardian Signature	Address
Witness Signature and Title	Address

III RESPONDING POLICE OFFICER

Name of Officer	Precinct	Shield No.	Precinct Complaint No.

IV PHYSICAL EXAMINATION

Time Begun a.m.　　p.m.	Has the patient bathed, washed or urinated since the suspected assault? YES ☐ NO ☐

Chief Complaint (In patient's own words)

Is the patient bruised? YES ☐ NO ☐ If "yes" describe:	Is the patient lacerated? YES ☐ NO ☐ If "yes" describe:	Has the patient any tender areas? YES ☐ NO ☐ If "yes" describe:

Note **ALL** other signs of physical trauma not covered by Pelvic/Rectal/Oral Examinations.

Note patient's blood type:

Pelvic/Rectal/Oral Examinations

Instructions:
1. Include **all** signs of trauma.
2. Note **size** and **development** of patient's organs, **bleeding, lacerations** and **tenderness.**
3. Speculum examination: Inspect cervix and vagina with a **NONLUBRICATED, WARM** speculum. A vaginoscope may be useful.

	FEMALE	MALE
GENITAL	Vulva: Vagina: Hymen: Cervix: Fundus: Adnexae Left:　　　　Right:	
RECTAL		
ORAL		

V LABORATORY SPECIMENS (EVIDENTIAL)

Take WET MOUNT of material from FORNIX and CERVIX. Examine this preparation IMMEDIATELY.

Note Findings:

Instructions:
1. Label all specimens collected for evidence with:
a. Patient's I.D. number
b. Anatomical location taken from
2. **PROPERLY PROTECTED SLIDES AND SWABS MAY BE PLACED IN THE SAME EVIDENCE ENVELOPE ALONG WITH ONE ARTICLE OF CLOTHING ONLY.**

Take at least 3 SLIDES of material: 2 from the VAGINAL POOL and 1 from the CERVIX. Allow sufficient streaking to permit analysis. ("Fix" slides. Label slides with a diamond pencil, place in protective containers and place in the EVIDENCE ENVELOPE.)

Were specimens taken?   YES ☐ NO ☐

Take SLIDES of material from any OTHER SUSPICIOUS AREAS as indicated. (e.g. other parts of the body including mouth and/or rectum) Allow sufficient streaking to permit analysis. ("Fix" slides. Label slides with a diamond pencil, place in protective containers and place in the EVIDENCE ENVELOPE.)

Were specimens taken?   YES ☐ NO ☐

Place SWABS used for streaking slides in the TUBES PROVIDED. (Label tubes with a diamond pencil, seal the open ends of the tube with tape over the cork. Initial tape with indelible ink. Place in the EVIDENCE ENVELOPE.)

Were swabs taken?   YES ☐ NO ☐

Clothing as Evidence

Instructions:
1. Articles of clothing may only be used as evidence if the patient consents to the release of evidence to the Police Department and/or the District Attorney's Office having jurisdiction on Part II of this form and if the patient consents to their relinquishment at the time of the visit.
2. Articles of clothing taken in conformance with 1. above must be labelled conspicuously with the patient's I.D. number.
3. IF MORE THAN ONE ARTICLE OF CLOTHING IS TAKEN AS EVIDENCE, EACH ADDITIONAL ARTICLE MUST BE PLACED IN A SEPARATE EVIDENCE ENVELOPE.

Place article(s) of clothing that may be sperm stained and/or used as evidence in the EVIDENCE ENVELOPE(S) after labelling.
Were such articles obtained?   YES ☐ NO ☐ Number of Articles:

Instructions:
1. The **EXAMINING PHYSICIAN** must **SEAL** the **EVIDENCE ENVELOPE(S)** and **SIGN** in the space provided over the flap also noting in the space provided the **NUMBER OF SLIDES, SWABS AND/OR ARTICLE OF CLOTHING** it contains.

VI TREATMENT RECORD

Was the patient given TETANUS TOXOID?
YES ☐ NO ☐

Was the patient given PROPHYLACTIC ANTIBIOTIC THERAPY? (e.g. for Venereal Disease)
YES ☐ NO ☐ Specify drug and dosage:

Was the patient given OTHER MEDICATION?
YES ☐ NO ☐ Specify drug and dosage:

Was the patient given a PREGNANCY PREVENTION DRUG?
YES ☐ NO ☐ Specify drug and dosage:

Was SURGICAL/LACERATION REPAIR required?
YES ☐ NO ☐ Describe in detail:

Was the patient given WRITTEN INSTRUCTIONS FOR VICTIMS OF SEXUAL ASSAULT?

YES ☐ NO ☐

Was the patient ADMITTED to the HOSPITAL?

YES ☐ NO ☐

VII REFERRAL

Will patient see PRIVATE PHYSICIAN for FOLLOW-UP CARE?
YES ☐ NO ☐ If "yes" complete the information required below.

Name	Address	Tel No.

VIII CONVEYANCE OF EVIDENCE

Instructions:
1. Place **SIGNED** and **SEALED EVIDENCE ENVELOPE(S)** in the **PLAIN MANILA ENVELOPE** with **COPIES 3 and 4 of the HOSPITAL REPORT—SUSPECTED SEXUAL ASSAULT FORM.**
2. Give the **PLAIN MANILA ENVELOPE** containing the **SIGNED** and **SEALED EVIDENCE ENVELOPE(S)** and **COPIES 3 and 4 of the HOSPITAL REPORT—SUSPECTED SEXUAL ASSAULT FORM** to **HOSPITAL SECURITY ONLY.**

Specimens Given to:	Name	Title	Organization

_____ M.D.
Examining Physician's Signature

THE PELVIC EXAMINATION: A VIEW FROM THE OTHER END OF THE TABLE

By Joni Magee, M.D.

(From Annals of Internal Medicine, October, 1975)

Lying on the examining table, feet in stirrups, confronting the examiner with the most personal parts of your anatomy, gives you plenty of time to think. Because I also perform pelvic examinations, I thought about what could be done to make me like them better. During the years certain parts of the procedure stood out as crucial. Speculum insertion is usually the most traumatic event in the examination. A detailed explanation of the sensations experienced and suggestions for alleviating some of them are presented. Other aspects of the doctor-patient relationship during the pelvic examination are explored and suggestions for improving patients' perceptions of them are offered.

One piece of advice I heard in medical school that I'll never forget came from the chief of surgery: Every surgeon should have a laparotomy once a year. His opinion, clearly, was that nothing improves doctor-patient rapport more than shared experience. During my myriad of pelvic examinations, instead of just looking at the ceiling, I thought a lot about why I didn't like most of them. After I became a resident in obstetrics and gynecology and was doing examinations myself, I got to understand exactly what the examiner was doing. What follows is the result of my supine ruminations.

I was once referred to the office of a world-renowned specialist for investigation of a problem with great emotional impact for me. My history was taken by one of the lesser lights, but the pelvic examination was to be done by the chief himself. I was taken to the examining room and positioned and draped in the usual manner, legs in stirrups, sheet over my knees so I couldn't see past them, my perineum exposed to whatever breeze might have been stirring. The great man entered the room, followed by two associates, and walked to the head of the table. There, towering over me, he extended his hand and introduced himself. I had a powerful urge to laugh hysterically, curse him, and kick him, but I smiled sweetly and said, "How do you do?"

Now, as they say on *Sesame Street,* "What's wrong with this picture?" Why did I react so violently? It took me years to figure out the reason was that a handshake and an introduction imply a meeting between equals. However, that postural relation, with me in that very undignified, ludicrous, but necessary position clearly implied that I was helpless; nowhere near equal. The whole scene was so ridiculous and demeaning that it was an extremely unpleasant experience. The moral of the story is that if you have arrived to do a pelvic examination, introduce yourself to your patient while she is still sitting up, preferably clothed, but, anyway, sitting up. It doesn't take very long for her to lie down, and she'll feel much more human and happy.

Then, there she is and there you are, sitting down there between her legs where she can't see you, getting ready to apply all sorts of unknown tortures. What do you do? Hum a little tune? Many examiners do nothing. That is, they say nothing. For your patient's sake, talk! Tell what you're going to do just before you do it. The shock value is greatly diminished that way. I usually say, "I'm going to touch the outside of your vagina and spread it apart. Now, I'm going to put my fingers in. Now, relax!" That is, I used to say, "Relax!" but I don't say it anymore. What is she supposed to relax? Her hands? Her toes? Her whole body? What you specifically want her to relax is the perineal floor, the levator ani muscle. But, if you tell her that, you won't get anywhere either. So, I tell her she has a muscle she squeezes closed when she has to go and can't get to the bathroom, and she should do the opposite of that. For good measure, you push down and out from just inside the introitus and tell her to relax the muscles you are pushing on.

Now, you ask, "What are you doing with your fingers in her vagina when the speculum examination comes first?" But first a word about speculums. Many patients call them "clamps." That evokes a frightening image. A rapid explanation that you're really not going to clamp anything soothes most jangled nerves. If you really feel like talking, you can even tell her what the speculum actually does. Next, they're cold, at least the metal ones are, and the plastic ones have other drawbacks. Anyway, lubricant spoils Papanicolaou smears and gonococcal cultures, so often you can't use lubricant with a speculum. But water doesn't spoil anything. And, if by some miracle there's some hot water around, you solve two problems at once by using it on the speculum. To actually insert this device, there are two methods. Because the introitus is vertical, it seems logical to insert the speculum in the anterior-posterior diameter and rotate it once it is inside. Before you do that, imagine someone's scraping a steel beam over your urethra. It's excruciating!

Back to your fingers. They allow a much kinder initial invasion than a cold, hard instrument. And while they are in the vagina, you can get a feel of the cervix so you know which way to point the speculum and how far in it needs to go. Then you put it in right over your fingers, being careful not to touch the roof of the vagina. You put it in *slowly*. *Very slowly*. Five extra seconds can prevent your patient from feeling like a rape victim. [Or, if the patient *is* a rape victim, five extra seconds can keep her from feeling assaulted again.—Editor.] Then, you open it. This is worth a special warning, such as, "You'll feel like you have to go

The pelvic examination: A view from the other end of the table

79

The pelvic examination: A view from the other end of the table

the bathroom both ways at the same time.'' If you're using a plastic speculum, it locks open with a very startling click, which causes less anxiety if the patient is forewarned. It clicks again when you release it.

When you insert your fingers for the bimanual examination, slowness is again very important for comfort. Watch the patient's face. Don't ask her if it hurts; she'll tell you by her expression. You'll avoid a lot of decisions about whether a pain is significant that way. If you asked me if it hurt when you were flipping my uterus around, I would say, ''Yes.'' Actually, it feels weird, rather than hurting. If the patient tenses up during a bimanual examination, the examiner's first reflex is to say, ''Relax!'' But, again, this doesn't communicate specifically what you want the patient to do. ''Make your belly soft so I can push it and feel what's underneath it,'' gives the patient the feeling that she is being told what's going on, and makes her more cooperative.

The key word is ''communicate.'' Not only does the patient have a right to know what you are doing to, and finding out about, her body, but being treated as worthy of this knowledge makes her more cooperative. I've heard of a very progressive medical school (I hope it's not apocryphal) where every male student is placed in stirrups and a strange female physician comes in, squeezes his balls, and leaves without saying a word. If you think that would make you feel hostile and insecure, you might understand why women are so ready to complain.

I learned my method of speculum insertion from a man and added some refinements of my own. I mention this because I don't want to imply that only a woman can, or should, be an empathetic gynecologist. But doctors only learn how patients feel by being patients or by listening to them. All patients who get pelvic examinations are women, so, open your ears, men. You'll never learn from personal experience.

80

Used with permission of the publisher and author.

MEDICAL REPORT FOR SEXUAL ASSAULT

PHYSICAL EXAMINATION

(Please note bruising, lacerations, or any other physical trauma sustained by patient)

(1) HEENT:

(2) CHEST:

(3) BREAST:

(4) HEART:

(5) ABDOMEN:

(6) EXTREMITIES:

(7) NEUROLOGIC:

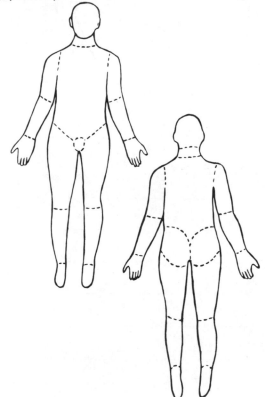

Signature of Physician

(8) GENITOURINARY: (describe external trauma)

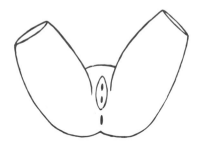

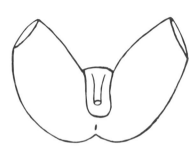

Wetmount: _____

IMPRESSION

_____

_____

_____

_____

_____

_____

_____

_____

Signature of Physician

A5

MEDICAL EXAMINATION RECORD

Suspected Rape			
		(Hospital Name) Receiving Ward	Brought by:
Name of Patient			Birthdate
Address			Age

AUTHORIZATION FOR RELEASE OF INFORMATION

I hereby authorize _____ to supply copies of ALL medical reports, including any laboratory reports, immediately upon completion, to the Police Dept. and the Office of the District Attorney having jurisdiction.

Person Examined _____

Address _____

Date _____   Parent or Guardian _____

Witness _____   Address _____

MEDICAL REPORT	Time arrived	Date & Time of Alleged Rape

History (as related to physician)

EXAMINATION	Date	Time

General Examination (include ALL signs of external evidence of trauma)

Laboratory Specimens Collected	Pelvic Examination (include ALL signs of trauma, size and development of female sex organs)
☐ Yes ☐ No (Mandatory, or explain absence)	
	Vulva
	Hymen
Date_____ Time _____	
	Vagina
Smears _____ Vulva	
	Cervix
_____ Vagina	
_____ Cervix	Fundus
	Adnexa (right)
Saline Washings _____ Vulva	
	Adnexa (left)
_____ Vagina	
	Rectal
(Laboratory Reports Attached)	Examining Physician

I hereby certify that this is a true and correct copy of the official _____ records
concerning the examination of the above named patient.   (Hospital Name)

Date   Title

HOSPITAL CONSENT FORMS AND PATIENT INSTRUCTION SHEET

CONSENT TO DISCLOSURE OF PRIVILEGED INFORMATION

(From Mt. Sinai Hospital, Minneapolis)

I, _____ hereby request and authorize Mt. Sinai Hospital and its attending physicians to disclose any information which has been acquired as a result of examinations, treatments, or tests upon me to _____ And in consideration of the services furnished to me I release Mt. Sinai Hospital and its attending physicians from any responsibility related to any disclosure of information or to any professional opinions, findings, or recommendations relating to the information as shown in the medical records.

Date _____
　　　　　Patient's Signature

Witness _____
　　　　　_____
　　　　　Signature of Parent or
　　　　　Guardian (if patient is a
　　　　　minor or ward)

Patient's Birthdate _____
　　　　　_____
　　　　　Signature of Nearest of Kin
　　　　　(if patient is physically
　　　　　unable to sign)

85

CONSENT FOR PHOTOGRAPHY

(From Harborview Medical Center, Seattle)

I, _____ hereby grant permission to be photographed while a patient of Harborview Medical Center. I understand that these photographs will become a part of my medical record.

_____
Patient's Signature

_____
Hospital Number

_____
Parent or Guardian

_____
Date

Witness:_____
Witness:_____
Date:_____

FOLLOW-UP FORM

(From Sexual Assault Center, Harborview Medical Center, Seattle)

INSTRUCTION
SHEET
FOR _____

An appointment has been made for you in _____
_____ Clinic.

On _____ at _____

It is important that you keep this appointment for follow-up care. Please call the number below if you have any problems before your appointment.

Please call the number for an appointment change or for advice, if you feel the need, especially:

1. If you experience emotional distress, or need help with the social or legal problems arising from this incident.
2. If you have signs of infection such as fever, pain, sores, discharge, etc.
3. If you have urinary symptoms such as frequent urination, pain on urination or difficulty urinating.
4. If there is any unusual vaginal bleeding.
5. If your menstrual period does not occur when expected, either normally or after hormonal therapy, if given to you. This should occur within seven (7) days after stopping the medicine.
6. If venereal disease tests have been done. Results are available four days after the tests at the number below. These tests should be repeated in two months. You have been given a laboratory request slip to take to the laboratory on the second floor.
7. If you have any questions about the instructions you have been given.

NUMBER TO CALL:
223-3047 8:30-5:00 Monday-Friday (Sexual Assault Center)
223-3074 Emergency Room (ask for social worker)

Hospital consent forms and patient instruction sheet

RAPE CRISIS COUNSELING INTERVENTION

EMERGENCY-ROOM RECORDS

All rape treatment emergency records should include a descriptive account of the trauma the victim has had, as well as factors that will be pertinent to his/her care in psychological and emotional follow-up in the center with the social worker. (The notes should be carefully written because they, like other records, may be subpoenaed.)

The record should include:
1. Age of the victim.
2. Race and nationality.
3. Marital status.
4. Who brought the patient to the emergency room.
5. Length of time between the trauma and presentation to the Rape Treatment Center.
6. Description of the episode:
   — Location
   — Identity of assailant known? If so, what was the relationship to the victim?
   — Use of alcohol or drugs
7. The victim's feelings at the time the counselor or nurse was with him/her.
8. Feelings the victim had regarding the rape.
9. Feelings the victim had regarding his/her self-image.
10. If the police were notified. If yes, what depart-

ment? If not, was an anonymous report completed by the victim?

11. Family members who are aware of the incident. What members does the victim not want to be notified?
12. Counselor's assessment of family and community supports.
13. Anxiety present and the degree of severity.
14. Counselor's evaluation of victim's ego strengths and coping mechanisms.
15. Assessment of the amount of future intervention the victim will need with the social worker in the center.

At present, we actively encourage the victim to return to the center for supportive counseling. The appointment slips are located in the center and are written in both English and Spanish.

COUNSELING PROCEDURES

I. Telephone Contact

A. During the day, the social worker will be responsible for answering the Rape Treatment Center "hot line" (325-7273). The emergency room will be responsible for the phone during the evening and night shifts. Only those persons who have been instructed in the proper treatment of rape victims will handle the rape calls. Other personnel may answer in the absence of a trained individual and take or give information that will allow contact between the victim and the appropriate staff member (i.e. take victim's name and number, give time when trained staff member will return call).

B. The person handling the call will:
1. provide initial supportive contact for the rape victim
2. ask for the date and time of assault and the name of the person calling
3. encourage the victim to come to the emergency room for treatment; give information regarding the services that will be provided
4. arrange transportation for the victim and ask if he/she wishes the police notified
5. ask the victim about physical trauma
6. ask the victim where he/she is located at the present time

All calls from the news media between 8 A.M. and 5 P.M., Monday through Friday, will be referred to the public information officer (ext. 6886). At other hours, on weekends and holidays, these calls will be referred to the administrator on call (beeper 251).

II. Emergency Room
A. When a rape victim arrives in the emergency room, the Rape Treatment Center social worker is notified by the emergency-room staff, Monday through Friday, from 10 A.M. to 6:30 P.M. During the other shift hours, the charge nurse and the nurse who has been trained and designated to handle the rape victims will be notified. The latter will stay with the victim through the complete process.
B. After reporting to the emergency room, the social worker/nurse counselor will:
1. assume case management for rape victim's mental health problems; provide immediate psychological support
2. contact police if victim so desires

3. arrange to contact relatives and/or friends if victim so desires
4. contact parent(s) or guardian of a minor
5. accompany victim during all procedures—including police questioning if case is reported to police—at the request of the patient or if counselor feels the support is necessary to the patient's welfare
6. counsel victim's family and/or friends if present and advise them concerning the victim's psychological needs
7. provide legal and medical information, to the extent permitted by the hospital, and advice, when detailed information can be obtained

C. When emergency-room procedures are completed, the social worker/nurse counselor will assess the case and discuss with the victim the availability of further psychological assistance. When circumstances warrant and the victim concurs, an appointment will be arranged for the victim to return. Appointments will be given for the earliest opening in the social worker's schedule. The victim should rarely have to wait longer than two days for a follow-up appointment. If physical trauma has incapacitated the victim, phone contact should be frequent, perhaps daily.

D. The social worker/nurse counselor should ensure that the victim has been given all information and has had all questions answered before the victim leaves. The victim should be given a phone number to call if problems arise between emergency-room discharge and appointment.

Rape crisis counseling intervention

III. **Counseling Aftercare**
   A. Within 24 to 48 hours, the victim receives a

Rape crisis counseling intervention

follow-up phone call or letter from the social worker to further assess the victim's condition. At that time, the social worker makes note of the victim's concerns and further directs him/her, if necessary.

B. The rape victim has counseling services available if desired, for as long as necessary, with the social worker at the Rape Treatment Center. If the patient requires extensive counseling, the social worker has resources available for further treatment.

C. The rape victim is also seen at the four-week check-up appointment by the social worker to determine if the patient needs further assistance.

Used with permission of Jackson Memorial Hospital, Rape Treatment Center, University of Miami.

RAPE CASES: IS YOUR TEST HANDLING FAIL-SAFE?

**By James A. Terzian, M.D., and
Bettina G. Martin, M.S., HT(ASCP)**

(From Medical Laboratory Observer, September, 1977)

Your hospital laboratory *must* be able to provide expert clinical evidence and testimony in cases involving an alleged rape. Here's why. Federal crime statistics show that 66,094 rape cases were reported in 1976 in the United States. The charges against many of the defendants in these cases were dismissed prior to trial. Less than 34 per cent of the rape cases that did go to trial resulted in convictions. What's going wrong? Many clearly guilty rapists may go free because laboratorians improperly collect or handle evidence that could lead to convictions.

An effort is now being made in hospitals all across the country to organize health teams that are expertly trained to collect clinical evidence from rape victims. All of us have a key part to play in this effort. We must be especially concerned with the chain of evidence that we collect. This chain is composed of a number of links, with each link representing a systematic procedure performed by a physician or laboratorian. The first link in this chain is forged when the victim seeks medical attention. The chain becomes complete after all lab reports have been verified, signed, and turned over to the hospital administrator.

We recently updated our protocol for maintaining the integrity of the chain of evidence in rape cases. Much of the initial work on this protocol was done by Ellie Bechtold, M.D. First we decided that we needed a locked box where reports and specimens taken from the victim could be stored when the clinical pathology attending physician or resident could not immediately examine them. We also needed special containers holding all of the forms and specimen collection equipment that must be readily available when a rape victim is physically examined. Our answer to both needs is the medicolegal lockbox.

Here's how our medicolegal lockbox system works. The attending physician uses the forms inside the box to take the patient's history, obtain signed releases, and order tests. A witness is always present throughout the examination. This witness should be a woman, preferably a nurse or a seasoned laboratorian. We follow these guidelines for obtaining specimens:

A primary laboratory objective in proving rape is verification that spermatozoa are present in cytological specimens taken from the patient. (Caution: All cytological specimens *must* be taken by aspiration, to protect spermatozoa from crushing and air-drying.) The presence of acid phosphatase in fluid specimens collected in the examination may be equally acceptable as legal evidence of rape.* In most cases, we also collect medically important smears and cultures for gonococci, and blood for VDRL and alcohol measurements.

The victim's undergarments and outer clothing may also contain important forensic evidence. Retain those portions of the patient's clothing that you believe contain male ejaculate. Label this evidence. Some police departments prefer to test this evidence in their own laboratories. In other areas, the investigating officer or the prosecutor may ask you to perform these tests. Check with your laboratory director if you are unsure of local requirements. Here's a tip: Do *not* fold or crumple these suspect garments. Seminal fluid becomes fragile after it dries and must be handled with great

*Schumann, G.B.; Badawy, S.; Peglow, A.; and Henry, J.B. Prostatic acid phosphatase. Current assessment in vaginal fluid of alleged rape victims. *Am. J. Clin. Path.* 66: 944-952, 1976.

CONTENTS OF THE
MEDICOLEGAL LOCKBOX

Forms

- Consent for pelvic examination
- Physician's record
- Release of information
- Clinical and anatomical lab requisitions to microbiology, immunology, chemistry, and cytology
- Confidential records envelope, pre-addressed to the hospital administrator
- A ballpoint pen to complete forms.

Specimen Collection Equipment

- Sterile medicine dropper for collection of infant cytology smears and secretions for acid phosphatase
- Plain microslides for cytology and gonococcal smears
- Diamond-tipped pencil for labeling microslides
- Paper clips to separate microslides in fixative
- Cytology fixative (95% alcohol)
- Cardboard slide holder for gonococcal smears
- Culture tubes for microbiology
- Plain blood tubes for chemistry (acid phosphatase)

Specimen Record Book

The following must be completed:

- Date and hour of examination
- Patient's name
- Physician's *printed* name
- Itemized list of all specimens, including the source of each specimen
- Signatures of examining physician and witness

**Rape cases:
Is your
test handling
fail-safe?**

care to insure verification of the presence of spermatozoa.

We forge another link in our chain of evidence by labeling each specimen with the victim's full name, the source of each specimen, the determination to be performed, and the date each specimen was taken. The clinical pathology resident distributes these specimens to the appropriate section of the laboratory. The technologist receiving the specimens signs for them in the specimen record book. A written report of these test results, verified and signed by an attending pathologist, is then delivered to the medical records department. Cytology reports are hand-carried to the hospital administrator's office.

The examining physician forges the final link in our chain of evidence. Each medicolegal box contains an envelope that is pre-addressed to the hospital administrator. The physician places in this envelope the victim's records, the consent form, and the release form. The envelope is sealed and then hand-carried to the hospital administrator's office, where it becomes part of the patient's confidential record.

Suppose the victim is examined at night, when the hospital is virtually deserted? All important medicolegal specimens and paperwork are locked inside the medicolegal box at the conclusion of the examination. We then place the medicolegal box in a secure area, insuring that the custody will remain unbroken until the hospital administrator and the lab crew arrive. The keys for these boxes, by the way, are kept in the locked narcotics cupboard in the emergency room, in a secured area of the clinical pathology director's office, and in the hospital administrator's office.

We have several of these medicolegal boxes available so that one of them can be brought back to the laboratory and replenished while others remain available for immediate use. The contents of each box are periodically checked and replenished by technologists or emergency-room personnel.

At our hospital, the clinical laboratory director and his supervisors are responsible for educating the staff as to the standard operating procedure for the proper handling of evidence in rape cases. A written protocol means nothing unless everyone on the staff fully understands the importance of safeguarding the chain of evidence. We periodically review this written protocol with the day, evening, and night staffs. Policy changes are similarly reviewed, with copies of these changes sent for posting in the hospital administration office and in the emergency room.

Our inexpensive medicolegal lockbox system is a legally sound approach for preserving a chain of evidence that may be used in court against an accused rapist. Knowing exactly how the system operates, our laboratorians are confident that they won't somehow interfere with the due process of law.

Used with permission of the publisher and authors.

Rape cases: Is your test handling fail-safe?

DALLAS PROGRAM: TREATING VICTIM AND EVIDENCE WITH CARE

In one episode of a popular television series, a man accused of rape goes free only because the evidence that would have convicted him is accidentally destroyed in the hospital emergency room.

By centralizing the examination and treatment of alleged victims of rape, the Dallas program assures proper care of not only the rape victim but also the rape evidence.

One of the program's originators is Dr. Charles Petty, Dallas County chief medical examiner and professor of pathology at The University of Texas Southwestern Medical School at Dallas. He is also director of the Southwestern Institute of Forensic Sciences, which includes the medical examiner's office and the county crime lab.

He says: "Prior to 1973, when our comprehensive rape program began, rape victims were brought to different hospitals helter-skelter by law-enforcement agencies. There was no guarantee whatsoever that a rape victim would be given prompt, sympathetic treatment or that the evidence obtained would be handled properly."

Now all rapes reported in Dallas County are processed by the obstetrics-gynecology emergency department of Parkland Memorial Hospital, the major trauma hospital in the county and the medical school's primary teaching facility. Attending physicians are all faculty members in UT Southwestern's OB/gyn department.

The program has resulted in one of the best rape prosecution and conviction records in the country. In Dallas

County in 1975 (the last year for which final figures are available) there were 127 indictments for rape. Of those, 110 pleaded guilty. Of the 17 that went to jury trials, 14 ended in convictions.

According to Dr. Irving Stone, chief of the physical evidence analysis section of the forensic sciences institute and an assistant professor of pathology at the medical school, "The suspect is usually going to plead guilty when you have really good physical evidence." Analysis also may show that a man accused of rape did not, in fact, commit the crime. Nobody wants to "shove an innocent man into jail."

One of a rape case's most fragile supports is the so-called "chain of evidence"—the care and custody of the physical evidence. The chain should be short, Dr. Stone explains, involving as few people as possible. A signed receipt must be obtained each time evidence is transferred from one person to another.

Of course the primary concern is to treat the victim as a patient, Dr. Stone adds. She's going through what may be the most traumatic experience of her life, and even if she was lucky enough to receive no permanent injuries, "she still has to face the emotional problems associated with rape and the ordeal of the trial."

When she is brought to the Parkland emergency room, her case is given a priority that is second only to those in life-threatening situations. A victim who is suffering apparent physical or emotional trauma is taken directly into the examining room. "Treatment of her injuries comes first," says Dr. Daniel Scott, professor of OB/gyn at the university. "She is also treated for venereal disease, and given the option of treatment against pregnancy. The second part, and truly the second part of the examination, is for the purpose of collecting physical evidence that will support or refute an allegation of rape."

But Parkland's examining physicians are highly trained

The Dallas Program: Treating victim and evidence with care

The Dallas Program: Treating victim and evidence with care

specialists who are sensitive to rape victims' needs. "We try to show them we are removed from the legal aspects of the alleged crime," Dr. Scott says. "We don't ask for the background or details that police will need later for the investigation. Our questions are confined to what is important to the medical history."

The rape program includes special training for both Parkland nurses and members of various law-enforcement agencies in the county. Another important part of the system is the Dallas County Rape Crisis Center, operated by the Dallas Women Against Rape. The center operates a 24-hour crisis line and provides immediate personal counseling for rape victims admitted to Parkland.

Partially due to these improvements in rape-victim treatment, the number of reported rapes in Dallas County is rising. In 1973, when the program began, 500 victims were examined at Parkland. By 1975 the number had risen to 675, and in 1976 to 730.

The Dallas rape program's key to success is the close coordination of the various state, county, municipal and private agencies dealing with rape.

Used with permission of The University of Texas Southwestern Medical School.

100

FOLLOW-UP PHONE CALL TO RAPE VICTIMS

Follow-up phone contact should be made by the counselor at 24 hours, 48 hours, one week and six weeks, or whenever else necessitated by the needs of the rape victim and her family. To facilitate this procedure, ask the victim for times and phone numbers where she can be reached; discuss with her how you should identify yourself should someone else answer the phone.

When you call for the first time, identify yourself, e.g.: "I'm _____. I was with you in the emergency room _____ (x days, weeks, months) ago and I'm calling to see how you're doing now." Ask the victim whether you may speak with her now or should call again at a better time. The counselor may decide to give the victim her home phone number, but this involves a careful consideration of how available the counselor can and wants to be.

If the victim says that she does not want to talk with you, ask her if she can say why she feels that way, but do not persist or be insensitive to the victim's reluctance. A possible reply is, "I guess I can understand that you could feel that way now. I called to see how you were feeling (to give results of tests, arrange follow-up tests, etc.). Talking about what you're going through usually helps, and I hope that you'll call me in the emergency room anytime you'd like to talk. I'd like to call you again in _____ (x days, weeks, months) to see how you're feeling then."

Always listen for the victim to state her concerns and try to follow her lead. However, as a general outline, you can proceed through the questions on the follow-up form.

Please complete and file the form immediately after the conversation.

Patient's name:_____Counselor:_____
Date:_____How long since rape occurred:_____

I. **Somatic Concerns**
   A. *24 hr., 48 hr., 1 wk.:*
      1. Record results of
         VDRL:
         UCG:
         GC smear and culture:
         Other:
      2. Ask whether she's taking medication and whether she's having any side effects such as nausea, fatigue, pain at injection site, vertigo, etc. Please record for each medication.
   B. *6 wks.:*
      Has the patient had follow-up VDRL _____ UCG _____ ? If so, did she go to private M.D. _____ YNH clinic _____ Other _____ ? If not, remind her to have tests and give facilities' phone numbers and addresses.
   C. How are you *sleeping?*
      Do you have trouble falling asleep?
      Do you wake up frequently throughout the night?
      Do you wake up earlier than is usual for you in the morning?
      Do you have dreams or nightmares about the rape? If so, what are they about?
   D. How is your *appetite?*
      Have you gained or lost weight? How much?

E. Have you had any *medical problems?* (Please note treatment, if any.)
Headaches?
Nausea?
Stomachaches?
Diarrhea?
Constipation?
Difficulty in swallowing?
Unusual vaginal discharge?
Other?

II. Emotional Concerns
  A. Do you feel back to normal yet?
  B. Do you feel sad or down more than usual?
  C. Are you more nervous than usual?
  D. Do you ever find yourself crying or trembling without knowing why?
  E. Do you sometimes think so much about the rape that it's hard to think about anything else?
  F. Are there things that you're afraid to do now?
  Going outside?
  Being in a crowd?
  Being alone?
  Other?
  G. Do you get along with people as well as before?
  H. Do you feel any differently about being with a man since you were raped?
  I. Have you had sex with a man since the rape?
  J. Has your enjoyment of sex changed any?
  K. How about your responsibilities: Do you think you can do your work as well as before?
  L. Do you have a job outside your home? If so, have you returned to work? What's that been like for you?

III. Social Concerns

A. Have you been able to talk to any friends about being raped? If so, how did they respond?

B. Have you shared your feelings with anyone in your family? If so, how did each respond?
Mother
Father
Siblings
Husband
Children

C. If *husband or boyfriend* was told, does it seem to you that he treats you any differently since you were raped? Has he seemed different himself? Has he had problems such as:
Difficulty at work?
Variable moods?
Physical complaints?

D. If *children* were told, does it seem to you that they treat you differently now? (Specify for each child and record age.)
Have you noticed any changes in any of your children? (Specify for each.)
Have any of your children had problems such as:
Difficulty in school?
Variable moods?
Fearfulness?
Physical complaints?

IV. Legal Concerns

A. Did you decide to press charges when seen in the emergency room? If so, have you had any second thoughts?
How do you feel you were treated by the police?
Do they have the rapist in custody yet?
Do you have a lawyer?

How has it been working with your lawyer?
Has a trial date been set?

B. If the trial has taken place, what was it like being in court?

C. If charges have *not* been pressed, have you had any second thoughts about pressing charges?

V. After the Call

Describe patient's responsiveness.

Record any other applicable information.

Used with permission of Yale-New Haven Hospital, Rape Counseling Team.

**Follow-up
phone call
to rape victims**

CRISIS INTERVENTION AND INVESTIGATION OF °FORCIBLE RAPE

By Morton Bard and Katherine Ellison

(From The Police Chief, May, 1974)

The traditional focus of the police has been on law enforcement: the solution of the crime and the apprehension of offenders. However, it has become almost a cliché to point out that analyses of the police function reveal that they have increasingly fallen heir (estimated to occupy between 80 and 90 per cent of their time) to an increasing array of important human service functions. Traditional training gives them few tools to aid them in performing these functions. If the police are to provide these services in a manner satisfactory both to the public and to the officer, it is essential to draw upon the knowledge in other fields related to human behavior. This does not mean that police officers should be psychologists or social workers, rather it means that they should combine knowledge from these fields with their own unique experiences and expertise to perform all aspects of their job with maximum effectiveness, safety, and satisfaction.

Both law enforcement and human service functions are combined in an officer's dealings with a victim of forcible rape. This paper will deal with ways in which the police can use psychological knowledge both to benefit rape victims and at the same time to enhance their ability to apprehend offenders and close their cases satisfactorily.

The handling of rape investigations with psychological insight not only benefits the victim in terms of future psychological functioning, but also results in greater job satisfaction for the officer. In addition, it has ramifications in a larger sphere: "The word gets around," and an image is projected of an authority with psychological and technical competence. This must lead not only to greater public cooperation but also to a greater sense of security for the public at large.

Crisis theory: the background

The body of psychological knowledge known as crisis theory is particularly useful in enlarging an officer's understanding of the victim's psychological state and reactions, of the way the victim views the situation, and of the officer's role in relation to the event.

Crisis theory had its origins in 1942 when a Boston psychiatrist, Erich Lindemann, and his colleagues from the Harvard Medical School became involved with the victims and the families of victims of the Cocoanut Grove fire.[1] This terrible nightclub conflagration, in which almost 500 lives were lost and many more people were badly hurt, had a major impact on the city of Boston.

Lindemann's work with survivors, their relatives, and friends produced many ideas about how to deal with victims in crisis. This work has been enlarged and elaborated on by other researchers in the field. Much of the work that has been done has dealt with people in psychiatric crises, while practical applications in other areas have been slower to develop. This paper will suggest that crisis intervention theory has particular relevance to the police especially in their interactions with the victims of crimes against the person, particularly the crime of forcible rape.

Crisis and its aspects

Crisis may be interpreted in a wide variety of ways, but common to most definitions is the idea that it is a turning

Crisis intervention and investigation of forcible rape

[1]Lindemann, F. Symptomatology and Management of Acute Grief. *American Journal of Psychiatry.* 101, 1944.

point in a person's life. It is a subjective reaction to a stressful life experience, one so affecting the stability of the individual that the ability to cope or function may be seriously compromised. Crisis comes in many kinds and degrees. An event that may be of crisis proportions for one person may have less effect on another, but there are some situations that may be considered crisis-inducing for any individuals who experience them.

Crime victimization is one of the most stressful events in life. While it is not usually seen in crisis terms, it has all of the qualities that make for crisis. People tend to react to crime with the behavior that one sees in other, more obvious, crisis-inducing situations.

As every officer realizes, people respond differently to being victims of crime. While highly personal reactions to stress make it difficult to suggest a formula approach to people in crisis, it is possible to define some aspects of a situation that will typically be perceived and reacted to as a crisis. It may be useful to discuss important characteristics of stressful situations that result in a crisis reaction.

A. Stress

1. *Suddenness.* Stressful life events that are sudden tend to have a crisis impact. When a situation comes on slowly, people are able to readjust their psychological defenses slowly to cope with it. The death of a loved one who has been dying slowly over months or years usually has less crisis impact than a sudden, unexpected death.

2. *Arbitrariness.* A situation that is arbitrary usually is experienced as a crisis. This is the sort of situation that seems unfair, capricious, highly selective; it seems to happen in a no-fault, "out of the blue" way, resulting in the "why me?" phenomenon. An out-of-control auto selectively hitting one pedestrian in a crowd is an example of arbitrariness.

3. *Unpredictability*. Closely tied to arbitrariness and suddenness is unpredictability. In everyone's life there are normal and predictable developmental crises for which one can plan: marriage, a new job, a school examination, elective surgery, or any number of other events that are stressful but that can be predicted as being such with greater or less accuracy. Crises that can be anticipated lend themselves to planning so that some of the severity of the impact may be reduced. On the other hand, there are those crises which cannot be predicted. They are precipitated by wholly unforeseen events such as natural disasters, serious accidents, or crimes. It is the unpredictable that further confounds and complicates the stressful event leading to a crisis reaction.

B. **Reactions to Stress**

1. *Disruptiveness*. A crisis reaction has the characteristic of disrupting normal patterns of adaptation. Normally all of us have defenses which operate all the time to preserve the sense of "self," that is, to protect the self against the normal ebb and flow of life's events. We stay on a pretty constant course that way. But under the impact of a crisis-inducing situation, those defenses are disrupted and functioning suffers. Sleeping and eating patterns may become disturbed, work inhibitions may develop, attention and concentration become difficult.

2. *Regression*. Often individuals regress, that is, emotionally they revert to a state of helplessness and dependence that characterizes an earlier stage of development. When in a crisis, an otherwise mature and effective person behaves almost like a child in seeking support and nurturing, guidance

and direction from those regarded as strong and dependable.

3. *Accessibility.* With characteristic defenses disrupted, individuals in crisis are extraordinarily open and suggestible. This provides a unique opportunity to affect long-term outcomes.

One of an individual's most basic needs at this time is to vent feelings—to be able to talk about what has happened, to "get it out of your system." At this point sensitive intervention can help the person work through turbulent feelings about the experience and can minimize the long-term damage to psychological functioning.

If there is insensitive intervention, the individual quickly regroups his defense mechanisms and attempts to use them, often in extreme forms, to deal with the crisis. The defenses, instead of being appropriate reactions to a crisis situation, might harden into inappropriate habit patterns. For example, a common defense mechanism found in victims of crime is repression; they "forget" what has happened to them and can give only the barest, most confused details to the investigating officer. (One psychological theory tells us that this forgetting is only apparent and that the events continue to influence behavior.) Victims may tend to become paranoid and to feel someone is following them, or that the environment is dangerous, or that the offender is lurking nearby, even when this is not possible. They may develop nightmares, compulsions, or excessive, unreasonable phobias. Such defensive reactions often hinder not only the initial investigation, but also the successful legal pursuit of the case when the offender is apprehended and the case comes to trial. The person who "can't remember," who refuses to leave his or her room, and who fears all strangers can hardly be an ideal witness.

The disruption that occurs with crisis may become apparent immediately or there may be a delayed reaction. A police officer often sees a victim of serious crime, such as rape, who seems calm and unconcerned at the time, but who, three or four weeks later, needs psychiatric treatment or hospitalization. She may even call the officer who investigated the case and complain of acute or chronic insomnia or phobias, or that she is depressed and cannot stop crying. Because crisis symptoms might not be evident immediately, the officer must always act as though the situation is of crisis proportions.

Characteristics of successful intervention

Given the elements that make for crisis, what are the basic elements that contribute to dealing successfully with a person in crisis? Specifically, what should a police officer do to help the person in crisis regain equilibrium while, at the same time, furthering his own work?

Police have several advantages as crisis-intervention agents. Those who have worked with the crisis concept have emphasized the importance of early intervention. Being on the scene early allows one to take advantage of the period when the victim's defenses are down, when he/she is open and accessible to authoritative and knowledgeable intervention. The police officer is there early simply because people in crisis turn first to the police, especially when the crisis is precipitated by crime. Because the officer is there first, actions taken can critically affect, positively or negatively, the victim's subsequent behavior.

Almost as important is the question of authority. Most professionals in our society are seen as authority figures and their ability to perform their duties is enhanced by this aura of authority. Because professionals are expected to be competent, those seeking their services act in ways that will facilitate this competency; for example, people listen and follow directions.

Some professionals have learned to take advantage of this public confidence. In the field of medicine, it is common knowledge that most of what a doctor cures has nothing to do with anything that is specifically wrong with people. At least 70 per cent of a general practitioner's time is devoted to functional disorders, i.e., with ailments that are basically psychological in origin. (Not unlike the 80 per cent of police time being concerned with noncrime functions.) What people are cured by is a kind of laying on of hands. The doctor has come to have enormous authority in the eyes of people, and they turn to him for the satisfaction of psychological as well as physical needs. In the course of his training, he learns how to use this authority to help patients feel better.

Similarly, a police officer has considerable authority, both real and symbolic. The officer is the symbolic representation of everything from parent to the state. This is especially so when people are in trouble; people turn to the police to help in all sorts of difficulty, from a cat on the roof, to disputes with landlord or spouse, to emergency illness, to rape and robbery. Trouble is the business of the police, and society grants them much authority to deal with it. They must learn to use this authority because their behavior toward the individual in crisis must have impact upon both short- and long-term adaptations of such people.

Is rape a sex crime?

It is common to regard rape as sex crime. However, there is reason to question this view. Indeed, looking at it in the traditional way may well create a set in the police investigator's thinking that is dysfunctional. That is, to regard the act primarily as sexual in nature may distort the view of investigating officers, giving them a sense that they are dealing with something that really belongs in the area of morality. If one looks upon rape as a crime against the person, one may be more disposed to see it as one would view other aggressive crimes, such as robbery, assault, etc.

The difference in point of view may have a significant

effect on the investigator's handling of the case. Despite the new morality, in our society sex is still a subject that is highly charged emotionally, and is difficult to deal with coolly and objectively. Even the most hardened officer, for example, often reports difficulty in dealing with the case of a child who has been sexually molested. The special feelings in our culture about sex are revealed by the fact that, in many states, laws dealing with sex crimes differ significantly from laws dealing with other crimes against the person. For example, a woman carrying a purse is ordinarily not considered to be "asking for" a mugging, but a woman in a short dress is often accused of "asking" to be raped. No other crime has such stringent corroboration rules or requires such blameless character and conduct on the part of the victim.

Recent research on rape[2] suggests that the intent of the offender is more often aggressive than sexual to prove his masculinity and invulnerability by scapegoating and degrading the victim. Contrary to popular belief, the average rapist probably is not someone for whom normal sexual outlets are unavailable. Often too, the crime may follow a fight with a mother, a girl friend or a wife, and be a displacement of hostility against that woman.

Rape in the context of crimes against the person

To understand the impact of rape, it would seem appropriate to examine it in the context of other crimes against the person as they are experienced by the victim. All crimes against the person can be said to be violations of the self[3] and, as such, precipitate crisis reactions.

A burglary is such a crisis-inducing violation of the self.

Crisis intervention and investigation of forcible rape

[2]Amir, Menachim. *Patterns in Forcible Rape*. University of Chicago, Chicago, 1971.

[3]The self is an abstract concept: Sometimes called ego. It is the sum of what and who a person feels he is. A large part of the concept of self involves the body and the way one feels about the body, but it also includes such extensions of the self as clothing, automobile and home. For example, this may be expressed in such ways as: "That's just the sort of house I'd expect him to have."

People usually regard their homes or apartments as representative of themselves. In an important symbolic sense, their homes are extensions of themselves. It is, in the most primitive sense, both nest and castle. Particularly in a densely populated, highly complex environment it is the place that offers surcease and security. Each nest is constructed uniquely: Each is different, just as individuals are different. When that nest is befouled by a burglary, it is not so much the fact that money or possessions have been taken, but more that a part of the self has been violated.[4]

In armed robbery, a somewhat more complex violation of self takes place. Here the violation of self occurs in a somewhat intimate encounter between the victim and the criminal. In this crime, not only is an extension of the self (property, money, etc.) taken from the victim, but he or she is also coercively deprived of independence and autonomy, the ability to determine one's own fate. That is, under threat of violence, the victim surrenders autonomy and control, and his or her fate rests unpredictably in the hands of a threatening "other." This kind of situation must have a profound ego impact.

Now let us go a step further on the scale of violation of self to assault and robbery. Here there is a double threat: the loss of control, the loss of independence, the removal of something one sees symbolically as part of his "self," but with a new ingredient. An injury is inflicted on the body, which can be regarded as the envelope of the self. The external part of the self is injured, and it is painful, not only physically, but also in ego terms. Victims are left with the physical evidence reminding them that they were forced to surrender their autonomy and were made to feel like less than adequate people . . . a visible reminder of their helplessness to protect or defend themselves.

---

[4]This explains the sense of feeling "dirtied" often expressed by burglary victims. The intent to degrade is borne out by the fact that many burglars leave behind wanton destruction, and even, sometimes, deposits of feces.

In this discussion we have moved from considering the implications of the violation of self as it relates to the extension of a person (burglary), to the loss of control and autonomy as well as part of the self (armed robbery), then to a consideration of the insult to the envelope of the self as well as the loss of autonomy (assault and robbery). Now to the ultimate violation of self (short of homicide[5]), forcible rape. In the crime of rape, the victim is not only deprived of autonomy and control, experiencing manipulation and often injury, but also intrusion of inner space, the most sacred and most private repository of the self. It does not matter which orifice is breached. Symbolically they are much the same and have, so far as the victim is concerned, the asexual significance that forceful access has been provided into the innermost source of ego.

From an ego-psychological point of view, this kind of forceful intrusion into interior space would have to be one of the most telling crises that can be sustained, particularly since it occurs in the context of the moral taboos which traditionally have surrounded the sex function. Indeed, to view rape as purely a sex crime encourages the search for possible sources of satisfaction in the experience for the victim. Actually, there is little opportunity for gratification in the context. For example, if one focuses only on the sexual, one would be tempted to minimize the effects of rape on women with considerable sexual experience. This is not the case. That is why promiscuous women or prostitutes, for whom sexual activity is certainly part of their normal adaptive pattern, will experience rape as a crisis. For all women the focus is upon the intrusion and the violation of self; even prostitutes, for whom sex is a commodity, there is a need to have a sense of control, a sense of autonomy. When this control is taken from any woman,

Crisis intervention and investigation of forcible rape

[5]Homicide, of course, is the ultimate violation of self. However, witnesses of the homicide or relatives of the victim are usually in a crisis state. The intervention techniques useful with the victims of crimes against the person are appropriate for use with these individuals.

her defenses will be incapable of protecting her ego.

Adding to the victim's distress over violation is her awareness of cultural myths about rape, leading to fears of how friends and relatives will react toward her, and perhaps feelings that she surrendered under duress, to a ''fate worse than death.'' In this fearful, disrupted state, she sometimes comes to the police.

Implications for the investigator

The implications of all this for police investigators are truly profound. If officers realize the crisis significance of rape and have an understanding of their role, they can be considerably aided in achieving a successful outcome of the investigation. Remember that an individual in crisis may be in a state of regression, and it is natural in such a state to try to defend the self by repressing the experience. While regression provides an opportunity for fostering a relationship with the victim, repression may inhibit the communication of significant information.

A case history of a rape situation

Let us examine an example of a more-or-less typical rape case[6] and the way it was handled. Of particular interest are some of the crucial situations, how the police handled them, what they did consistent with our understanding of crisis theory, and how they might have responded differently.

One Saturday afternoon an 11-year-old girl, living in a large apartment complex in New York City, was accosted by a 16-year-old boy as she went into an elevator, was forced at knife point to the top of the building, and raped in the stairwell for half an hour. She was injured rather badly. When he left, she went down to the playground where she had been playing table tennis, picked up her racket, and

[6]Contrary to public expectations, the majority of victims of rape are in their teens, and younger victims are common. Parenthetically, young male victims of sodomy are not uncommon either.

dazedly commented on the experience to two of her little girl friends, then went to her own building, took the elevator to her family's apartment, and told her mother, who called the police. The police arrived quickly, questioned the family and the child with official demeanor, took the facts, and advised the family that detectives would be there shortly to conduct an investigation. They then advised a hospital examination and, indeed, took the child and her mother to the hospital.

About two hours later, two detectives arrived, asked essentially the same questions that the original officers had asked, told the parents they would be in touch, and left.

Then the problems began. The child tried to talk about the event as the evening went on and both mother and father conspired to keep her from talking about it. The mother experienced the event as having somehow been her fault. She had not protected her child, did not go down to the playground with her, did not keep an eye on her, etc. The father was enraged and guilty because he too had somehow failed to protect the child. There was a 15-year-old brother in that family who was also thrust into a state of crisis and was being ignored. Why was he in a state of crisis? It was an event that had involved sex, about which adolescents are particularly concerned. There was not much age difference between the two children; they were of different sexes and there must have been some feelings. After all, incest taboos operate strongly in all families. And, additionally, the victim had reported that the rapist was about the same age as her brother. Thus the situation must have had serious implications for him.

What we see here is an incident in which the crime of rape has produced a crisis not only for the victim but for the entire family as well.[7] The impact of the crisis, its shatter-

Crisis intervention and investigation of forcible rape

[7]This must be so in all cases, even if the victim does not tell her family about the crime; the changes that will almost inevitably be produced in her behavior as a result of the crisis will become obvious to those close to her. They will wonder what is wrong and be upset by these changes for which they can see no reason.

117

ing effects, the regressive tendency of all members of this family cry out for a firm, gentle but knowledgeable authority who, by his actions, can satisfy the need for support and strength. And if this authority is a police officer, he can at this time set the basis for furthering his investigation.

For example, the parents might be approached in the following way: ''Look, we're police officers; we've had experience with this sort of thing, and we understand. So let's talk about what our experience tells us is going to happen as a result of what's gone on here. You're going to feel more guilt than you may realize about what's happened to your little girl. You're going to ask yourselves, 'What could I have done to prevent this?' Well, in reality, you didn't do anything wrong, and neither did she, and there probably was nothing you could have done to prevent it. But we realize that knowing this is so doesn't keep you from feeling guilty all the same, and we understand that.''

Just such a simple statement gives the message that this person with authority is knowledgeable and understanding and can actually predict and give voice to the gnawing internal experiences of these parents. Somehow this process is not only reassuring but encourages trust and an openness with the officers.

From there the investigators might go on to anticipate their future reactions so that the family and/or the victim can recognize them and deal with them as they occur. At the same time, they may set the basis for furthering the investigation. They might say something like, ''We know that this is painful for the family, too. You're probably going to have a tendency not to want to hear about it, to feel that it would be best for everybody if your child didn't talk about it. But our knowledge in these situations tells us that people have a compulsive need to talk about what has happened to them, to 'get it out of their system,' to share it with someone who understands and who won't judge her, be harsh with her or blame her and says in effect, 'We still love you.'

Crisis intervention and investigation of forcible rape

118

"Now, I want you to do a job for us. I would like you to listen to what she has to say, and if at any time in the retelling of the story there is a new piece of information you didn't hear before, write it down, and call us immediately."

In other words, these officers would not only be demonstrating to the family that they know what they are doing, but they have also given them a job to do in relation to the event. They have made them partners in apprehending the offender. The family members can feel that they can do some good in the apprehension, and at the same time they are doing the most helpful thing they can for the victim.

From the viewpoint of the investigating officers, this may seem the long way around. It implies that they should not try to get more than the barest facts at first, that the original report by the patrolman first on the scene probably is enough to begin with, and that probing at this point, especially aggressive probing, is more likely to be harmful and impede the flow of information.

So we would suggest that the first interrogation or interview be a very general one, a helpful one, one that demonstrates to the victim and her family that the officer is concerned about them. The emphasis is on the victim and on her family, not on the offender . . . not yet. First the victim must be allowed to "pull herself together," then she will be willing and able to deal with cooperating in the process of apprehending the offender. A realization of this priority establishes a relationship that will serve as a basis for gaining information. The investigators might even set up an appointment and say, "We'll be back next Wednesday, and we'd like to talk to you then and see how things are going. Maybe then you'll feel a little differently, and will want to go into the matter a little more." The situation is defined as one of helpfulness, not force, and the victim will repay with information and cooperation because the officers gave her and her family the support they needed in crisis.

So more information is likely to be gained with a little

increase in time spent by the investigators. They have established a relationship of trust with the victim and her family. Their desire to help reciprocally will also lessen the likelihood that if a suspect is arrested, the victim will refuse to cooperate, or that her family will put pressure on her to forget the whole incident.

Further guidelines for investigation

We have attempted to present here a broad outline of how the theory of crisis intervention may be related to work with victims of rape. This outline has emerged from a blend of psychological theory and the practical experience of officers with whom it has been discussed. In discussing this outline with police officers who have dealt with rape cases, several more specific questions about the best procedures have arisen. In answer to the most common questions, some general guidelines may be presented that seem appropriate for the majority of cases. It is up to investigators, however, to realize that each situation differs and to use their discretion and intuition in determining when these suggestions are appropriate.

1. It is critical that the investigator scrupulously avoid any suggestion of force. This is especially true if the officer is male (and of course, most officers *are* male). Often, in his zeal to complete an investigation, because he is committed to what he is doing and really involved, the officer may be perceived by the victim as aggressive and forcible. In a sense, he is acting toward her essentially as the rapist had acted. The implication is obvious.
2. It is crucial that an authoritative investigator present himself in a benign, nonjudgmental way. This is especially true for the male officer. He must have patience and attempt to create a climate that will allow the individual to bring the information to the

surface willingly and naturally. The extra time that this seems to take will yield more information because it tends to short-circuit repression.

3. The officer should encourage the victim to talk about what has happened, even though he may find it painful and threatening to have to listen. He may want to probe gently in a later interview for information that may be particularly shameful to the victim or that she may not know how to express. This is particularly true if some form of sexual abuse or sodomy has or may have occurred. The officer may say something like, "Very often women tell us other things happened to them, too, things they consider unnatural or find hard to talk about. Did anything like this happen to you?" The officer must be careful, at the same time, not to suggest things to a victim who may lie or remember incorrectly in an effort to please him. A very gentle approach may prevent the tendency to induce suggested conformity.

4. The most appropriate place for interrogation differs with the circumstances. No relationship or encounter occurs in a void. It happens in a setting and the setting often determines what happens in it. Generally, the home is the best place for an interrogation, especially if the rape did not occur there and the victim has not expressed a desire that her family not know about the crime. The home is the extension of the self, and if the interview can be done privately, within the home, it often adds to the victim's sense of safety and security. If the officer is in doubt it often is appropriate to ask, "Where would you feel most comfortable talking about this?" The station house usually is the worst place. It is an environment that is conducive to neither the sense of comfort nor ease.

5. The question of place leads to the problem of the presence of others, and the necessity, often, of dealing with the family as well as with the victim. Most victims are part of a social network, and their reactions to a crisis will affect the way they relate to others, whether the others are told about the crisis or not. A victim may be afraid to tell her husband about the rape, but he cannot help but notice that her behavior has changed, that something is wrong, and this will, in turn, influence his behavior toward her, often in ways that make the crisis worse.

6. The victim always should be seen privately. Even the most well-meaning relative or friend will be upset by the situation and will try to cut off the victim's need to ventilate. If the interview is in the home and the family members seem particularly anxious, it is sometimes helpful to interview the other members of the family first. This should be done without the victim in the room and for the purpose of assuring family members that both they and the victim are blameless. It is important that the authority make clear that the victim acted correctly because she is still alive. It is important, too, to reflect for them something of what they are feeling. They then may be enlisted as helpers in the investigative process.

7. If the victim comes to the station house alone to report the crime, she may want and need support in dealing with her family. It is appropriate to ask if she would like to be taken home and have the officer help her explain the situation to her family. At any rate, given the nature of the social view of this crime, the meaning the crime has for the victim (i.e. violation of self), and the effect upon the person, it is very important that the privacy of the relationship with that immediate authority be un-

complicated by any other relationship. It should be developed in the context of confidentiality and closeness. If the officer establishes a good relationship with the family so that they understand the crime and its significance to the victim, they have a way of dealing with the situation. This enables them to relate to the victim with the same sense of compassion and understanding that they have just received.

8. In later interviews, the officer assigned to the case may help the victim by de-mystifying the court procedure. He may also give her the names of organizations that have been formed to help the victims of rape. In New York City, for example, members of women's organizations familiar with the court procedure are available to supportively accompany the victim through the complexities of the legal process.

9. A frequently asked question is whether the officer assigned to the victim of a rape should be male or female. The reality in most police departments in this country is that the bulk of work is done by male officers. Even if one wanted to refer the victim to a female investigator, such an officer may not be available. If the victim specifically and spontaneously requests a female officer, every attempt should be made to provide one for her. However, there is some feeling that there are advantages to having a sensitive male officer deal with the case. An understanding, supportive male at this time may help the victim overcome a natural aversive reaction to men. That is, she sees, at a time when such an experience is vital, that not all men are aggressive and harmful. This may ease her job of relating to the other men in her life. In any case, more important than the sex of the investigator is the

individual officer's crisis-intervention and investigative competence.

Summary

In this brief presentation we have attempted to place the crime of forcible rape in the context of crisis theory. An understanding of human crisis and of crisis intervention techniques by an investigating police officer can immeasurably aid the rape victim in preserving her psychological integrity and also aid the investigating officer in the apprehension of the offender and in the preparation of a case that will stand up in court.

Crisis intervention
and investigation
of forcible rape

INTERVIEWING THE RAPE VICTIM

(From the International Association of Chiefs of Police, 1974)

The interview of a rape victim requires exceptionally intimate communication between the police officer and a victim who has been physically and psychologically assaulted. As such, the investigative nature of the interview represents only one dimension of the officer's responsibility. By conducting the interview tactfully and compassionately—and with an understanding of the victim's psychological condition—the officer can avoid intensifying the victim's emotional suffering. At the same time, the cooperation of the victim is gained and the investigative process is thereby made easier.

Law enforcement authorities agree that, for many reasons, rape is the most underreported crime in the United States. Because of its highly personal nature, many victims are too embarrassed to report the crime. They would rather forget the incident than discuss it. In some instances, the rapist may be a relative or family friend, and therefore the victim is reluctant to file a complaint. Some victims do not contact the police because they fear that the investigative, medical and prosecutorial procedures followed in a rape case are as psychologically traumatic as the crime itself.

The legal process that the rape victim encounters is unfamiliar to her and, under the circumstances, emotionally threatening. The police interview, in which the victim necessarily relives the crime by giving a detailed account of the rape and answers intimate questions, is followed by the courtroom trial where she can be subjected to an intimidating cross-examination by the defense lawyer. The legal process may take years, constantly reminding the victim of the experience and making her relive it each time.

As the initial step in the legal process, therefore, the police interview should be more than an investigative inquiry. It should also be used to acquaint the victim with the complicated legal and medical system she will encounter.

Important to the successful interview is the officer's understanding of the emotional condition of a rape victim. When interviewing a victim, the officer should not regard rape as solely a physical sexual assault. He should consider the psychological effects rape has on its victim. Often the lasting scar of rape is an emotional one, leading to marital problems, mental illness—even suicide.

Legal elements of rape

According to common law, there are three elements to the crime of rape when the female is over the age of consent: carnal knowledge (penetration), force and lack of consent.

Penetration, as an essential element of rape, means that the sexual organ of the male entered and penetrated the sexual organ of the female. Court opinions have held that penetration, however slight, is sufficient to sustain a charge of rape. There need not be an entering of the vagina or rupturing of the hymen; the entering of the vulva or labia is all that is required. During the interview, the officer must clearly establish that penetration occurred with the penis. Penetration by use of a finger is not rape, although it is, of course, another form of assault.

The victim must have resisted the assault, and her resistance must have been overcome by force. The amount of resistance that the victim is expected to have displayed depends on the specific circumstances of the case. The power and strength of the aggressor and the physical and mental ability of the victim to resist vary in each case. The

126

amount of resistance expected in one case will not necessarily be expected in another situation. It can be expected that one woman would be paralyzed by fear and rendered voiceless and helpless by circumstances that would inspire another to fierce resistance. There must be real, not token or feigned, resistance on the part of the woman before there can be a foundation for a rape charge.

Although there is no universal accord as to what degree of resistance is necessary to establish the absence of consent, the generally accepted doctrine is that a female, who was conscious and possessed of her natural mental and physical powers when the attack occurred, must have resisted to the extent of her ability at the time. Resistance is necessarily relative and the presence or absence of it depends on the specific facts and circumstances. Some women will have been so terrified that there will be no physical signs of resistance.

The kind of fear that would render resistance by a woman unnecessary to support a case of rape includes a fear of death or serious bodily harm, a fear so extreme as to preclude resistance or a fear that would render her incapable of continuing to resist. On the other hand, consent, however reluctant, at any time prior to penetration deprives the intercourse of its criminal character of rape. There is, however, a wide difference between consent and submission: Consent may involve submission, but submission does not necessarily imply consent.

In the absence of a statute requiring corroboration, common law generally holds that the unsupported testimony of the victim, if not contradictory or incredible, is sufficient to sustain a conviction of rape. Some states, in order to provide safeguards against unfounded accusations of rape, have laws that require corroborative evidence. Corroboration is supportive evidence that tends to prove that a crime was committed. It lends credence to the allegation that the crime occurred and needs not to be proved beyond doubt.

Interviewing the rape victim

It is incumbent upon the police officer to obtain all possible corroborating evidence even if there is no statute requiring it. Corroboration of a rape offense can take physical forms such as semen stains on clothing, bruises, cuts and medical evidence of intercourse. It can be circumstantial, such as statements and observations of witnesses.

Although in some jurisdictions rape can be proved by the sole testimony of the victim, it is not common. Medical and scientific evidence is of prime importance and will frequently directly influence the successful prosecution of a rape case.

Psychological reactions of victims

That rape is intrinsically a crime of physical violence is explicit in its legal definition—"the having of unlawful carnal knowledge by a man of a woman, forcibly and against her will."[1] That it is more than that, however, is apparent from the reactions of rape victims, who in many cases sustain more psychological damage than they do physical injury.

SELF-CONCEPT: Except for homicide, rape is the most serious violation of a person's body because it deprives the victim of both physical and emotional privacy and autonomy. When rape occurs, the victim's ego or sense of self as well as her body is penetrated and used without consent. She has lost the most basic human need and right: control of physical and emotional self.

Perhaps most damaging to her self-concept is the intrusion of her inner space. Psychologically, it does not matter which orifice has been violated. Symbolically, breachment of any one represents a forced entry into the ego.[2]

[1]Anderson, William S., Ed., Ballentine's Law Dictionary. The Lawyers Co-operative Publishing Co., Rochester, N.Y., p. 1054.

[2]Morton Bard and Katherine Ellison, "Crisis Intervention and Investigation of Forcible Rape," Police Chief (IACP; Gaithersburg, Md.) May 1974, p. 71.

Police officers should be aware that the rape victim has been forced to experience an event that, from her viewpoint, is emotionally asexual. The victim's psychological response to rape primarily reflects her reaction to violation of self. As such, it is extremely important that police officers view rape as an emotional as well as a physical assault.[3] This is true regardless of the moral reputation of the victim. Even prostitutes will experience the psychological violation of self when raped.

RESPONSE TO INTERVIEW: The way in which rape victims respond to the interview situation varies, depending on their physical condition and individual psychological makeup. Victims can range from quiet and guarded to talkative. Some victims find it extremely difficult to talk about the rape, perhaps because of the personal nature of the subject or because they are uncommunicative while under pressure. Others find relief in discussing the details of the rape. Often a victim will exhibit both patterns during the course of an interview.

The two verbal patterns frequently displayed by rape victims during an interview are indicative of general emotional states that are commonly associated with the psychological effects of rape. The victim may respond to the crime in an expressed manner; that is, she verbally and physically exhibits fear, anger and anxiety. Or, the victim may respond in a controlled behavior pattern by hiding her feelings and outwardly appearing to be calm, composed or subdued.

A number of rape victims will show their feelings through physical manifestations. Crying, shaking, restlessness, tenseness—all are means of expression that accompany discussion of the crime, especially the more painful details. Some women may react by smiling or laughing to avoid their true feelings. Comments such as "really, nothing is wrong with me" combined with laughter serve as a

Interviewing the rape victim

[3]Ibid., p. 71.

substitute for the distressing memory of the attack.

Rape victims who are composed and able to calmly discuss the rape are usually controlling their true feelings. Presenting a strongly controlled appearance during a personal crisis may be the way they habitually cope with stress. In some cases, however, the victims' state of calmness may result from physical exhaustion rather than a conscious effort to remain composed. Because many rapes occur at night, victims are frequently exhausted, not having slept since the previous night.

A silent reaction on the part of the victim may also be encountered. The officer needs to realize that silence does not mean that the victim is hiding facts. It does mean that she is having a difficult time in starting to talk about the incident.

Another emotional reaction of rape victims is to express shock that the incident occurred. Statements such as "I can't believe it happened," "It doesn't seem real" or "I just want to forget it" are common psychological responses to the trauma of rape.

Although there is no doubt that general emotional reactions to rape vary among individuals, there does seem to be one common psychological denominator: fear. Experienced police officers have often observed that the victim feared for her life during the rape, that she viewed the rapist as a potential murderer. In most cases, the emotional reaction to this fear does not dissipate by the time of the interview.

Regardless of the victim's emotional reaction and its observable manifestations to the crime, the interview itself creates additional anxiety. In many cases, the victim is totally ignorant of police procedures; perhaps she has never before talked with a police officer. The only certain thing is that she will have to discuss with a stranger the details of what is probably the most traumatic experience of her life. This produces a conflict within the victim: She *knows* that to make possible an investigation, the details of the rape must be discussed, but she *feels* apprehensive about describing the experience.

The character of the emotional stress that the victim experiences when she describes the rape is perhaps frequently misunderstood. To recount the details of the rape, the victim must mentally relive the incident. In most cases, the victim's psychological defenses will interfere with her ability and desire to remember what occurred. The victim may not be able to recall certain parts of the attack, or she may consciously change certain facts or omit them. The officer must exercise great patience and understanding in eliciting from the victim the necessary details of an experience she does not want to relive. Officers need to realize that this reliving of the experience, if not properly handled, can amount to a psychological rape of the victim.

Another important factor is that the interview should be thoroughly conducted. The officer should gather complete information during the in-depth interview; thus he avoids the need to repeatedly question the victim at later dates. This constant re-interviewing in effect requires the victim to relive the experience again and again. To avoid repeated interviews, the officer must overcome some victims' difficulty and reluctance to talk by conducting a structured interview.

The interview

The investigative goal of the police officer in interviewing a rape victim is to determine if and how the crime occurred. From the statements made by the victim to the officer the essential elements of the offense and the direction of the investigation are established.

Because the interview process may be considered as a routine operation, the police officer may, if not careful, project the feeling of not being concerned with the victim as a person. The danger is that the victim may be left with the

Interviewing the rape victim

impression that she is being treated as an object of physical evidence rather than as a person. The officer cannot allow this to happen. It is during the personal and sensitive communication of the interview that the victim's cooperation is gained and her emotional well-being is maintained. If the officer treats the victim impersonally, he will not gain her confidence and the interview will be unsuccessful. The officer may also cause the victim further emotional stress.

OFFICER'S ATTITUDE: When interviewing a rape victim, the officer must realize that, from the victim's viewpoint, what has occurred has not only been a violent sexual intercourse but also a perverted invasion of her self. Further, the officer must be constantly aware of his own sexual attitudes and the subtle and not so subtle ways in which they emerge. Special care should be exercised so that the rape victim is not placed in the position of perceiving herself as being guilty because of the personal nature of the crime and the social stigma attached to it. A professional bearing throughout the interview will help the officer obtain an accurate report of the crime without causing the victim to experience unnecessary anxiety.

PHYSICAL COMFORT: It is unreasonable to expect a rape victim to respond to detailed questioning while she is uncomfortable or in physical pain. The victim may have been beaten as well as raped. Frequently, the rape has occurred outdoors, and the victim and her clothing have been soiled. Sometimes the victim has been urinated on or has been forced to commit oral sex. Under conditions such as these, the preliminary interview should be brief, and the in-depth follow-up interview should be conducted after the victim has been medically treated, and her personal needs such as washing and changing clothes have been met.

SETTING: The interview should take place in a comfortable setting where there is privacy and freedom from distraction. A place such as a crowded office is inappropriate. A rape victim finds it difficult to discuss the intimate details of the crime with the interviewer; her reluctance to talk will greatly increase if there are other people present. She should be isolated from everyone, including friends, children, husband, boyfriends and other victims.

It is often desirable that a policewoman conduct the interview. In some incidents, particularly with a juvenile, a rape victim can more easily discuss the crime with a woman than with a man. Frequently, however, no female officer is available. Nevertheless, the police should consider the presence of a trained female, such as a nurse or social worker, to help ease the victim's embarrassment and anxiety.

OPENING REMARKS: To most rape victims, the interviewing officer is not just a police officer. The officer is also an official representative of society, probably the first representative met during a legal process that traditionally has placed a moral burden on rape victims. As such, the officer may symbolize to the victim the entire society. His behavior may represent to the victim the general attitude of the community toward her plight. If the officer is callous, accusatory in manner or speech, the victim may leave the interview fully expecting society—and perhaps even her family—to react in the same way. In addition, the victim may begin to question her own motives and therefore feel unnecessary guilt.

At this critical point, when the officer should presume that his attitudes are being expressed to the victim, he must gain her confidence by letting her know that a major part of his function is to help and protect her. He should make plain his sympathy for and interest in the victim. By doing this, the officer contributes to the immediate and long-term emotional health of the victim. He also lays the foundation of mutual cooperation and respect on which is built the effective interview.

"VENTILATION" PERIOD: Following the opening remarks, the officer should allow the victim to discuss whatever she wants. This ventilation period gives the victim an opportunity to relieve emotional tension. During this time, the officer should listen carefully to the victim, but he should be aware that any initial description of the incident may be colored by the trauma of the experience. Everyone's perception of reality is altered by extreme stress.

INVESTIGATIVE QUESTIONING: After the necessary ventilation period, the victim should be allowed to describe what occurred in her own words and without interruption. As the victim tells the story of the rape, she will also tell a great deal about herself. Her mood and general reaction, her choice of words and her comments on unrelated matters can be useful in evaluating the facts of the case. It is important in such an interview that the police officer be humane, sympathetic and patient. He should be alert to inconsistencies in the victim's statement. If the victim's story differs from the originally reported facts, the officer should point out the discrepancies and ask her to explain them in greater detail. The officer should phrase his questions in simple language, making sure that he is understood. It is best if the questions are presented in a manner that encourages conversation rather than implies interrogation.

Often the rape victim will omit embarrassing details from her description of the crime. Officers should expect a certain amount of reluctance on the part of the victim to describe unpleasant facts. The officer should explain that certain information must be discussed to satisfy the legal aspects of rape and pursue the investigation. He may add that the same questions will be asked in court if the case results in a trial.

In a majority of cases the attack is premeditated, and about half the time the rapist has known or has seen the victim before the assault. Because of this, certain questions should be asked.

The victim should be asked if, and how long, she has been acquainted with the offender. The circumstances of their meeting and the extent of their previous relationship, including any prior sexual relations, should be discussed. Although previous sexual acts with the accused will not absolve the offender at this particular time, knowledge of them helps to establish the validity of the complaint. Along these same lines, the officer should determine if the victim has ever made a charge of this nature in the past; review of previous records, if any, will provide insight into the present complaint.

Where it is determined that the victim had known the rapist prior to the incident, he should be identified and interviewed. If the offender is unknown, the officer must get a detailed description of him including clothing, speech and mannerisms. The officer should determine whether the offender had accomplices or revealed any personal facts such as area of residence or places he frequented. Questions such as "Was anyone else present when first meeting or being attacked by the rapist?" should be asked. Did the offender use a weapon? What type? What kind of vehicle did he drive? After obtaining all the possible information about the unknown rapist, the officer will begin his search.

INTERVIEW'S END: As a result of having been raped, some victims suffer long-range emotional problems. At his discretion, the police officer may suggest that the victim seek assistance from an appropriate counseling agency, family physician, psychologist or clergyman. In addition, the officer may explain to the victim's family the emotional suffering rape victims typically encounter.

Summary

From the information given by the rape victim during the interview is developed the investigative direction of the case. Without these facts, as personal and unpleasant as they always are to recount, police investigation of the crime cannot proceed.

The manner in which the interview is conducted is vital to the emotional health of the victim. The police officer should be aware that the rape victim has been assaulted psychologically as well as physically. In conducting all phases of the interview, he should keep the well-being of the victim uppermost in his mind by acting tactfully and compassionately.

Interviewing the rape victim

A DISTRICT ATTORNEY'S RAPE COORDINATION PROJECT

I'll begin meeting with hospital liaisons this week. The suggested conference subject matter is outlined below. These discussions will also be used to explain the rape coordination project, and to indicate the seriousness with which our office views the crime of rape.

The purposes of these primary meetings are as follows:
— To describe procedures we will follow to minimize inconvenience to medical witnesses.
— To describe procedures the liaisons should follow to ensure minimal inconvenience to hospital personnel and to preserve evidence.
— To determine extent of ancillary hospital resources.

A. **District attorney procedures**
1. Give hospital personnel as much advance notice of district attorney involvement as possible.
2. Request medical records only when necessary.
3. Give the witness an adequate pretrial briefing.
4. Consider witnesses' medical and personal obligations in arranging pretrial conferences.
5. Give witnesses an opportunity to review the record before meeting with the assistant district attorney.
6. Take medical witnesses out of order at trial, for their convenience, when effective trial strategy will not be compromised.

B. Liaison procedures

1. Request medical personnel to record all patient statements. The patient's exact words should be used to describe symptoms. Quotation marks around the patient's words will distinguish them from the recorder's conclusions. This permits the record to speak for itself, and aids the assistant district attorney's comparison of statements.

2. Request medical personnel to record statements by other persons. All statements should be verbatim and identified by informant's name. For example: "Patient's mother said, 'Alice came home soaked with blood around the genital area.' "

3. Request medical personnel to record the date and time of each entry.

4. Request medical personnel to record the scope of the physical examination. When the patient complains of localized trauma, the examiner should:
   — record complaint in patient's words;
   — make physical examination of the area;
   — record examination findings.

5. Request medical personnel to make records legible. Legibility applies to contents of entries *and* signatures. Illegible records require the testimony of the recorder at trial. In addition, photocopies provided must be legible, and nonstandard abbreviations should be avoided.

6. Request medical personnel to sign all entries, even when a page contains more than one entry.

7. Prohibit the use of crime-victim records for instruction of medical personnel. This office recognizes the value of reciprocal legal-medical education in the professions. However, such records' evidentiary value can be severely compromised by gratuitous observations of persons not fully trained. In addition, it may be necessary to have the trainee

appear in court to explain the records' entries.

8. Obtain medical records, requests for which will come from the assistant district attorney, for trial. Review the records to ascertain that each entry is legible and signed. Where illegible, the entry must be reviewed by liaison and recorder. Thereafter, a certified, typed, verbatim transcription—signed by both liaison and original recorder—must be attached to the record. A certified copy of it should be forwarded to the district attorney's office or it may, in some cases, be picked up by a process server or detective.

9. Obtain medical witnesses. The district attorney's office will advise liaison as soon as the need for medical testimony becomes apparent. Liaison will contact the witness and make the original record available for his review. Thereafter, the witness will phone us for a briefing on the case. If necessary, a pretrial conference will be arranged, at the mutual convenience of the witness and the assistant district attorney, to discuss:
— the nature of the case;
— why the witness's testimony is required;
— scope of witness's testimony and, especially, reasons for limitations thereon;
— courtroom procedures.

This office will place medical witnesses on subpoena standby, a procedure that will be explained to the liaison in advance, and to the witness during his initial briefing. The standby subpoena will be made out to the physician but sent to the liaison, who will get advance notice by telephone of all subpoenas being prepared. In special instances, we will arrange transportation for medical witnesses. Where possible, witness will be presented at court out of order where scheduling difficulties arise.

A district attorney's rape coordination project

139

C. Ancillary hospital resources

We will determine if each health-care facility has, or can develop, resources for:

— blood analyses;

— semen analyses;

— marshaling and analyses of foreign matter (hairs, skin under fingernails, etc.) removed from the patient;

— immediate treatment of rape victims in emergency rooms;

— psychological counseling for rape victims.

Used with permission of Richard Stefan Lurye, Assistant District Attorney, Queens County, New York.

SAMPLE PHYSICIAN TESTIMONY

Direct examination

Prosecutor: Doctor, were you in your office in the late afternoon or early evening of _____?

Witness: I was.

Prosecutor: Did it happen that day, sir, that a young woman named _____, accompanied by some other people, came to your office?

Witness: Yes.

Prosecutor: Did you conduct a physical examination of _____?

Witness: I did.

Prosecutor: Did you have an opportunity to observe her physical condition?

Witness: I did.

Prosecutor: Would you relate to the jury what her physical condition was at the time?

Defense Attorney: Excuse me, Mr. Prosecutor, what was the time?

Prosecutor: Late afternoon, early evening. Do you, Doctor, recall the exact time she came to your office?

Witness: I recall it was approximately five o'clock. I don't recall the exact time. But the complainant was brought in at that time by a number of police officers, and I was asked to examine her. She was evidently in a good deal of discomfort but very cooperative and certainly lucid. She did her best to try to help me to accomplish a good examination. I examined her at that time and found by means of speculum examination that there were live motile sperm at the vault of the vagina. At the time, smears were made for gonorrhea. She was also given an injection of progesterone and estrogen so that she would not conceive. At that time I also noticed some ecchymosis, which is bruising, around the vaginal opening and the perineum, which is that part of the anatomy next to the vagina.

Prosecutor: Did you see bruises anywhere else?

Witness: I didn't examine her entire body but fairly much confined myself to the area that allegedly had been attacked.

Prosecutor: In conducting your internal examination, Doctor, do you recall whether or not you observed a hymen inside the vagina?

Witness: Yes, there was an intact and distensible, easily distensible hymen.

Prosecutor: What does that mean?

Witness: The hymen was soft and could easily be displaced, but there was an intact hymen.

Prosecutor: Would the presence of such an intact hymen be consistent with penetration?

Witness: Oh, yes. Since speculum examination or examination with a metal instrument was accomplished, certainly penetration could have occurred with the hymen intact as it was.

Prosecutor: So the record is clear, your examination disclosed the presence of live spermatozoa in the vagina?

Witness: Yes. I made smears in the office.

Prosecutor: Did you view them yourself?

Witness: I did them myself, and I saw them. My office nurses were witness to them.

Defense Attorney: I move to strike all this, what his nurses saw.

The Court: Yes, strike it out.

Prosecutor: You saw them?

Defense Attorney: Your Honor, I have no dispute about the doctor's testimony. Doctor, all I want to know is: Did you view the slides yourself?

Witness: Yes, I viewed the slides myself.

Prosecutor: Thank you. No further questions.

Cross-examination

Defense Attorney: Blood can be typed, can it not? There are various types of blood?

Witness: Yes, of course.

Defense Attorney: Is there any way to identify spermatozoa?

Witness: I believe people skilled in forensic medicine can type tissues and spermatozoa and so forth.

Defense Attorney: In other words, it's possible—is it not, Doctor—for the spermatozoa that you took from that girl to have been classified or typed and measured against or compared with someone else's spermatozoa? Is that possible?

Witness: I think that should be answered by a forensic specialist.

The Court: You may answer it.

Witness: The slides I made and submitted to the police officers, who took them along with them, could even at this late date be typed. This,

143

much like other blood work, would not necessarily show that someone was the attacker but might exclude someone. That's possible. But nevertheless I turned those over to the police officers, and if they chose to type them, that would have been their mission. I had no equipment by which to do it in my office.

Defense Attorney: I have no further questions.

Redirect examination

Prosecutor: Doctor, have you ever typed semen?

Witness: No, I have not.

Prosecutor: Do you know how easy or difficult it is to type semen?

Witness: To someone who's an expert at this . . .

Prosecutor: Do you know?

Witness: No, I do not. I have no expertise in this.

Prosecutor: You have never done it before?

Witness: I have not.

Prosecutor: So you do not know at this late date if semen can be typed?

Witness: I know it can be.

Prosecutor: In any instances?

Witness: I don't know.

Prosecutor: You have no personal experience in this.

Witness: I do not.

Recross-examination

Defense Attorney: Doctor, from your knowledge of the literature on the subject, it could have been typed at or around the time that you took the smears, had the police resorted to a forensic specialist, isn't that so?

144

Prosecutor: Your Honor, I object to the question. It's too speculative.

The Court: I'll allow it.

Witness: In all sincerity I'd have to say I have no personal expertise at this. I would have to call in my consultants in a matter of this sort to determine whether or not this is so. I'm a gynecologist, and this would be within the province of someone who is more a clinical pathologist.

Defense Attorney: You testified during my cross-examination that spermatozoa can be classified or typed, isn't that so?

Witness: Well, I've heard of it being done.

Defense Attorney: And the district attorney asked you whether it could be done at this late date, and at that point you said you didn't know, is that right?

Witness: I'm not sure whether this specimen could be done at this late date. I can tell you that according to former City Coroner _____ various things could be done at late dates. I don't know if this specimen could be done.

Defense Attorney: You mean a year or so having elapsed from the time you took the smear, is that right?

Witness: Well, in the time that elapsed from the time I took the smear, yes.

Defense Attorney: Did any police officer who accompanied this woman ask if you could or would either type the sperm yourself for purposes of identification, or send it to a consultant?

Witness: No.

Prosecutor: Objection, Your Honor.

The Court: Overruled. Let me ask you a question, Doctor.

In order to classify sperm, you'd have to have something to compare it with, would you not?

Witness: No, sir. It isn't like that. Well, yes. I guess they would have to have typing serum.

The Court: Is this like blood—I mean, where a person is born with a certain type blood and has that type blood throughout his life?

Witness: It is like that, yes. They would use a typing series.

The Court: But in order to compare something, you must compare it with something. You can't compare something with itself, can you?

Witness: Well, yes. They would use a typing serum. They would not use a donor specimen.

The Court: But in order to determine the individual from whom this sperm originated, you would have to have that individual available, am I correct?

Witness: That would be true, yes, absolutely.

Defense Attorney: Well, if, at the time of the event on _____, you didn't have an individual to compare it with, that wouldn't stop you on that day from classifying the sperm, waiting until the alleged perpetrator was apprehended, and then comparing a sample from him, isn't that so?

Prosecutor: I object to the question, Your Honor. I think it's improper for this witness.

The Court: We're bordering on the theoretical here. This doctor has already told us this was not his area of expertise. Doctor, I assume whatever testimony you're giving in this field is on the basis of your reading rather than actual use as a physician?

Witness: Yes, sir. I have never had occasion to utilize it as a physician, and this is really on the basis of

	my reading and professional conversation, but no personal experience whatever.
The Court:	We'll accept your statement that you're not an expert in the field.
Defense Attorney:	But you are familiar with the literature?
Witness:	Yes.
Defense Attorney:	And you have discussed this on a professional basis with your colleagues, have you not?
Prosecutor:	I object to what his discussions are, Your Honor.
Witness:	I don't recall any discussions.
Prosecutor:	Your Honor . . .
The Court:	He said no. You want the answer stricken?
Prosecutor:	I would like to have the complete line of questioning stricken from the record. He's not an expert in the field.

Sample physician testimony

147

COMPARISON OF STAFFING AND WORKLOAD IN SELECTED SEX CRIME INVESTIGATIVE UNITS

Department/ investigative unit	Female population[1]	No. of rapes[2]	Per 100,000 females
St. Paul Sex-Homicide Unit	165,071	92	55.7
San Diego Sex Crimes Detail	337,790	173	51.2
Seattle Morals Unit	276,438	276	99.8
Minneapolis Sex Division	235,555	236	100.2
Oakland Assault Detail	187,868	220	117.1

Other crimes investigated[3]	Staff	Working hours[4]
All crimes against the person except robbery	1 captain 9 sergeants	9:00 a.m. to 9:00 p.m. (over-lapping shifts)
Sex-oriented assault and kidnapping, child-molesting, indecent exposure, some homo-sexual cases	1 sergeant 3 detectives 2 policewomen	7:00 a.m. to 4:00 p.m.
All sex crimes	1 sergeant 4 or 5 detectives	7:00 a.m. to 3:45 p.m.
All sex crimes	2 lieutenants 2 special investigators	Daytime
All sex crimes	2 sergeants 1 policewoman	8:00 a.m. to 4:00 p.m.

149

Staffing and workload in selected sex crime units

Department/ investigative unit	Female population[1]	No. of rapes[2]	Per 100,000 females
Ft. Lauderdale Homicide Division	73,973	75	101.4
Tucson Sex Crimes Detail	136,330	84	61.6
St. Louis Sex Offense Investigative Unit	338,769	565	166.8
District of Columbia Sex Offense Branch	405,019	596	147.2
New York Area Sex Crimes Squad	4,191,507	3,735	89.1
Los Angeles Investigative Divisions	1,459,437	2,146	147.0

Other crimes investigated[3]	Staff	Working hours[4]
All crimes against the person except robbery	1 detective-sergeant 4 detectives	Daytime, called out at night for homicide & rapes
All sex crimes	1 sergeant 3 investigators	8:00 a.m. to 4:00 p.m., on call 24 hrs./day
All sex crimes	1 sergeant 10 patrol officers	24 hrs./day
All sex crimes	1 captain 2 lieutenants 4 sergeants 24 investigators	24 hrs./day
First degree sex crimes and attempts	1 lieutenant 2 sergeants 23 investigators per squad (4 squads)	8:00 a.m. to midnight. Sex Crimes Analysis Unit female police officers voluntary reserve system operates at night.
Variable according to division size	Variable according to division size (17 divisions)	24 hrs./day (Specialists work daytime hours)

Staffing and workload in selected sex crime units

151

Staffing and workload in selected sex crime units

Department/ investigative unit	Female population[1]	No. of rapes[2]	Per 100,000 females
Los Angeles County Sheriff's Detective Bureau	3,630,256	736	20.3
Chicago Homicide Sex Units	1,764,285	1,619	91.8

[1]1970 Census figures. Information obtained from the U.S. Bureau of Census, Statistical Information Branch.
[2]All figures taken from "Uniform Crime Reports," 1973.

Other crimes investigated[3]	Staff	Working hours[4]
Variable according to station size	Variable according to station size (16 stations)	24 hrs./day
All crimes against the person except robbery	1-2 sex crimes specialist investigators in each of 6 areas	24 hrs./day

[3]"All sex crimes" excludes prostitution and other forms of vice.
[4]These figures do not reflect the immediacy of the response; some units respond as soon as possible, others respond as late as 24 hours later.

Staffing and workload in selected sex crime units

PROTECTIVE MEASURES TO PREVENT RAPE

PERSONAL SAFETY TIPS FOR WOMEN

At home

1. Women who live alone should list only last name and initials in phone directories and on mailboxes.
2. The best lock cannot function if you fail to lock it. Be sure you lock your doors during the day, even if you are home and even if you only leave it for a few minutes (to walk the dog, get the mail, etc.).
3. Never open the door automatically after a knock. Require the caller to identify himself satisfactorily; this includes repairmen, delivery men and policemen. Use chain bolt when checking identification.
4. Have adequate lighting at all entrances—front and back. Inside and outside lighting provides a good measure of protection.
5. If you are going out for the day and will not return until after dark, use timers to activate your lights and give you added safety. Have your key ready so that you can open the door immediately.
6. When a stranger asks to use your phone, do not permit him to enter. Offer to summon emergency assistance or make the call for him.
7. If a window or door has been forced or broken while you were absent, do not enter or call out. Use a neighbor's phone immediately to call the police, and wait outside until they arrive.

Driving

1. When practicable, travel on well lighted, populated streets and thoroughfares. Keep windows and doors locked.
2. Keep car in gear while halted at traffic lights and stop signs. If your safety is threatened, hold down on the horn and drive away as soon as possible.
3. Check your rear view mirror. If you believe you are being followed by another car, do not drive into your driveway or park in a deserted area. Pull over to the curb at a spot where there are people, and let the car pass you. If the car continues to follow you, drive to the nearest place where you can get help (gas station, police station, fire house, etc.).
4. If you should be followed into your driveway at night, stay in your car with the doors locked until you can identify the occupants or know the driver's intent. Sound horn to get the attention of neighbors or scare the other driver off.
5. When parking at night select a place that will be lighted when you return. Look around for loiterers before leaving the car.
6. Never leave car keys in the ignition, even if you are parked only for a short time. Take them with you, and make sure the car is locked.

Walking

1. After getting off a bus or leaving a subway station at night, look around to see whether you are being followed. If someone suspicious is behind you or ahead of you, cross the street. If necessary, criss-cross from one side to another, back and forth. If you feel you are being followed, don't be afraid to run. (One of the criminal's greatest assets is his ability to surprise you, to attack when you least expect it, by suddenly leaping

Protective measures to prevent rape

155

out and not giving you a chance to fight back.) Should he continue to trail you, be prepared to defend yourself by screaming and running to a lighted residence or business or to flag down a passing car.

Protective measures to prevent rape

2. If a car approaches and you are threatened, scream and run in the direction opposite that of the car (the driver will have to turn around to pursue you).
3. Walk near the curb and avoid passing close to shrubbery, dark doorways and other places of concealment. Shun shortcuts, especially through backyards, parking lots and alleyways.
4. Have your key ready in hand, so your house door can be opened immediately.
5. When arriving home by taxi or private auto, request the driver to wait until you are inside.

Elevators

1. If you live in an apartment where you know the other residents and find yourself in the lobby with a stranger, you can let him take the elevator and wait for it to return for you.
2. If you are on the elevator and someone gets on whose presence makes you uneasy, get off at the next floor.
3. Always stand near the control panel; if attacked, hit the alarm button and press as many of the other buttons as you can reach with your arm or elbow. The elevator will then automatically stop at every floor pressed, a procedure that your assailant would have difficulty reversing.

CHECKLIST FOR VICTIMS

1. Report the crime immediately to the police.
2. Do not wash or douche as you will receive medical treatment.

156

3. Submit to a medical examination and treatment as soon as possible.
   — Inform the doctor of the exact acts committed and have him note any evidence of these acts.
   — All injuries or bruises, even if minor, should be noted and treated.
   — Have semen smears taken from all areas where penetration occurred.
   — Inquire as to treatment for venereal disease and pregnancy.
4. Inform the police of all details of the assault, and of anything unusual you may have noticed about the assailant. Every detail is of extreme importance, as it can lead to an arrest that will prevent other innocent persons from being assaulted.
5. Give all stained or torn clothing to the police. Especially important are undergarments.
6. Advise the police of any other information you may recall at a later date.
7. You are under no compulsion to answer any questions from persons not associated with the investigation. Refer persistent inquirers to your investigator.

Used with permission of the Newark, N.J., Police Department.

Protective measures to prevent rape

COMMUNITY ANTIRAPE PROJECTS

The list below was adapted and expanded from a list first compiled during 1974-1975 by the authors of *Rape and Its Victims: The Response of Citizens' Action Groups*. The centers are listed alphabetically by city under the appropriate state. Some addresses and phone numbers may have changed since then. However, once an antirape center is established and known to the community, location changes are usually avoided.

The National Organization for Women (NOW) has rape task forces in almost 200 chapters around the country. Information about them is available through the NOW Action Center, 425 Thirteenth St., N.W., Room 1048, Washington, D.C. 20004 (202) 347-2279.

The National Center for Prevention and Control of Rape (part of the National Institutes of Mental Health) has compiled a rape program directory. A free copy may be obtained by writing the Institute at 5600 Fishers Lane, Rockville, Md. 20857.

ALASKA

Fairbanks Crisis Line
Fairbanks, Alaska 99701
(907) 452-4403

ARIZONA

Center Against Sexual Assault
Box 3786
Phoenix, Arizona 85003
(602) 257-8095

Assault Crisis and Prevention Center
P.O. Box 26851
Tempe, Arizona 85282
(602) 257-8095

ARKANSAS

Rape Crisis, Inc.
P.O. Box 5181
Hillcrest Station
Little Rock, Arkansas 72205
(501) 375-5181

CALIFORNIA

Bay Area Women Against Rape
P.O. Box 240
Berkeley, California 94701
(415) 845-RAPE

Rape Information and Prevention Center
San Fernando Valley Free Clinic, Inc.

P.O. Box 368
Canoga Park, California 91303
(213) 888-6515

Women Against Sexual Abuse
12818 Morningside Avenue
Downey, California 90242
(213) 653-6333

Rape Crisis House
127 W. Main Street
El Cajon, California 92020
(714) 444-1194

Rape Emergency Assistance League
of San Diego County
P.O. Box 468
El Conjon, California 92022

Feminist Task Force
Rape Crisis Service
P.O. Box 368
Fairfield, California 94533
(707) HER-AIDE

South County Women's Center
Rape Crisis Center
c/o 25036 Hillary
Hayward, California 94544
(415) 537-2112

Marin County Rape Crisis Center
P.O. Box 823
Kentfield, California 94904
(415) 924-2100

L.A. Commission on Assaults Against Women
P.O. Box 74786
Los Angeles, California 90002
(213) 653-6333

Women Against Rape
c/o River Queen Women's Center
P.O. Box 726
Monte Rio, California 95462
(mailing address)
17140 River Road
Guerneville, California 95446
(street address)
(707) 869-0333

Mid-Peninsula WAR
c/o YWCA
4161 Alma Street
Palo Alto, California 94306

Stop Rape, Inc.
P.O. Box 651
Placentia, California 92670
(714) 525-HELP

Sacramento Women Against Rape
Sacramento Women's Center
1221 20th Street
Sacramento, California 95814

(916) 447-RAPE
(916) 442-6161 (office)

Rape Crisis Service
c/o Family Service Agency
1669 N. ''E'' Street
San Bernardino, California 92405
(714) 886-4889 (24-hr.)

San Diego Rape Crisis Center
P.O. Box 16205
San Diego, California
(714) 239-RAPE

San Jose Rape Crisis Center
YWCA
375 S. 3rd Street
San Jose, California 95112
(408) 287-3000

Harbor Free Clinic
615 S. Mesa
San Pedro, California 90731
(231) 547-0202

Santa Barbara Rape Crisis Center
1220 Santa Barbara Street
Santa Barbara, California 93101
(805) 963-1696

COLORADO

Rape Counseling Service
P.O. Box 2518
Colorado Springs, Colorado 80901
(303) 471-HELP

York Street Center
1632 York Street
Denver, Colorado 80210
(303) 388-0834

Denver Anti-Crime Council
1313 Tremont Place, Suite 5
Denver, Colorado 80204
(303) 893-8551

Denver Coalition on Sexual Assault
227 Clayton Street
Denver, Colorado 80206
(303) 355-5510

Denver Victim Crisis Line
c/o Southeast Denver Neighborhood
Services Bureau
227 Clayton Street
Denver, Colorado 80206
(303) 321-8191 (crisis)
(303) 321-1793 (office)

Rape Prevention Program
Department of Psychiatry
Denver General Hospital
8th and Cherokee
Denver, Colorado 80204
(303) 623-8252

**Community
antirape
projects**

159

Community Crisis and Information Center
202 Edwards Street
Fort Collins, Colorado 80521
(303) 493-3888

Pueblo Rape Crisis Center
509 Colorado Avenue
Pueblo, Colorado 81004
(303) 545-RAPE (24-hr.)
(303) 545-8271 (office)

CONNECTICUT

Bridgeport Rape Crisis Service
YWCA
1862 E. Main Street
Bridgeport, Connecticut 06604
(203) 334-6154

People Against Rape
448 Birch Road
Fairfield, Connecticut 06430
(203) 366-0664

Hartford Sexual Assault Service
YWCA
135 Broad Street
Hartford, Connecticut 06105
(203) 525-1163

Neighborhood Women Against Rape
P.O. Box 14272
Hartford, Connecticut 06114

Prudence Crandall Center for Women
P.O. Box 895
New Britain, Connecticut 06050
(203) 229-6939

Rape Crisis Center
c/o Women's Center
Cor. Broad Street & Williams
New London, Connecticut 06320
(203) 443-1425

DELAWARE

Rape Crisis Center of Wilmington
901 Washington Street
Wilmington, Delaware
(302) 658-5011

DISTRICT OF COLUMBIA

D.C. Rape Crisis Center
P.O. Box 21005
Washington, D.C. 20009
(202) 333-RAPE

Feminist Alliance Against Rape
P.O. Box 21033
Washington, D.C. 20009

FLORIDA

Rape Information and Counseling Service
P.O. Box 12888

Gainesville, Florida 32604
(904) 377-RAPE

Community Relations Commission
350 Bay Street
Room 406
Jacksonville, Florida 32202

Hubbard House
Jacksonville Rape Crisis Center
1231 Hubbard Street
Jacksonville, Florida 32007

Women's Rape Crisis Center
P.O. Box 10572
Jacksonville, Florida 32207
(904) 384-2234

Rape Treatment Center Emergency Department
c/o Jackson Memorial Hospital
1611 N.W. 12th Avenue
Miami, Florida 33136
(305) 325-RAPE
(305) 325-6901

Hillsborough County Stop Rape, Inc.
P.O. Box 1495
Tampa, Florida 33601
(813) 228-RAPE

GEORGIA

Rape Crisis Center
Grady Memorial Hospital
Atlanta, Georgia 30303
(404) 659-1212 (X-4460)

Carroll Crisis Intervention Center
201 Presbyterian Avenue
Carrollton, Georgia 30117
(805) 963-1696

Mayor's Commission on the Status of Women
501 Running Avenue
Fort Benning, Georgia 31905

ILLINOIS

Women's Development Council
1751 Felten, Apt. 3
Aurora, Illinois 60505
(312) 851-3675
(312) 897-4241

Feminist Action Coalition
Southern Illinois University
Washington Square "a"
Carbondale, Illinois 62901
(618) 536-2103

Women Against Rape
1001 S. Wright
Champaign, Illinois 61801
(217) 384-4444 (crisis)
(217) 344-0721 (office)

Chicago Coalition Against Rape
c/o ACLU
5 S. Wabash, Room 1516
Chicago, Illinois 60603
(312) 236-5564

Chicago Legal Action for Women
Northside Rape Crisis Line
5609 N. Broadway
Chicago, Illinois 60660
(312) 728-1920

Chicago Women Against Rape
37 S. Wabash
Loop Center, YWCA
Chicago, Illinois 60603
(312) 372-6600

Emma Goldman Women's Health Center
1317 W. Loyola
Chicago, Illinois 60626
(312) 262-8870

DuPage Women Against Rape
Box 242
Clarendon Hills, Illinois 60514
(312) 629-0170

INDIANA

Indiana University Police Department
428 N. Lansing
Indianapolis, Indiana 46205
(317) 264-7971

Women United Against Rape
Indianapolis Anti-Crime Crusade
5343 N. Arlington Avenue
Indianapolis, Indiana 46226

Women's Committee on Sex Offense
P.O. Box 931
South Bend, Indiana 46624
(219) 282-2323

IOWA

Ames Hotline
Box 1150
Iowa State University
Ames, Iowa 50010
(515) 292-7000

Women's Counseling Service
310 W. 3rd Street
Davenport, Iowa 52802
(319) 322-1719

Iowa Women's Political Caucus
P.O. Box 1941
Des Moines, Iowa 50306
(515) 282-8191

Polk County Rape/Sexual Assault Care Center
700 E. University
Des Moines, Iowa 50316

(515) 262-4357 (24-hr.)
(515) 283-5666

Iowa City Rape Crisis Line
c/o Women's Center
3 E. Market Street
Iowa City, Iowa 52240
(319) 338-4800

KANSAS

Lawrence Community/University of Kansas
Rape Victim Support Service
220 Strong Hall
University of Kansas
Lawrence, Kansas 66045
(913) 864-3686

Manhattan Rape Crisis Center
Kansas State University
Center for Student Development
Holtz Hall
Manhattan, Kansas 66506
(913) 532-6432

KENTUCKY

Rape Relief Center
c/o YWCA
604 S. 3rd Street
Louisville, Kentucky 40202
(502) 585-2331

LOUISIANA

Rape Crisis Center of Baton Rouge, Inc.
P.O. Box 65037
Baton Rouge, Louisiana 70806
(504) 383-RAPE
(504) 383-7273

Stop Rape Crisis Center
414 Louisiana Avenue
Baton Rouge, Louisiana 70801

YWCA Rape Crisis Service
3433 Tulane Avenue
New Orleans, Louisiana 70119
(504) 488-2693

MAINE

Rape Crisis Center
335 Brighton Avenue
Portland, Maine 04102
(207) 774-3613

MARYLAND

Baltimore Rape Crisis Center
128 W. Franklin Street Rm. 103
Baltimore, Maryland 21201
(301) 366-7273

Rape Action Center, Baltimore County
Sheppard Pratt Hospital
6501 North Charles Street

Community antirape projects

Windy Brae, Room 103
Baltimore, Maryland 21204
(301) 321-7273

Prince George's County
Sexual Assault Center
Prince George's General Hospital
Cheverly, Maryland 20785

University Women's Crisis Hotline
Health Center
University of Maryland
College Park, Maryland 20742
(301) 454-4616

Montgomery County Sexual Offenses
Committee
Commission for Women
64 Courthouse Square
Room 5
Rockville, Maryland 20850

Passage Crisis Center
Montgomery County Health Dept.
8500 Colesville Road
Silver Spring, Maryland 20910
(301) 589-8610

MASSACHUSETTS

Everywoman's Center
Goodel Hall
University of Massachusetts
Amherst, Massachusetts 01003

Rape Crisis Intervention Team
Beth Israel Hospital
330 Brookline Avenue
Boston, Massachusetts 02215
(617) 734-4400 (X-2179)

Alliance Against Sexual Coercion
P.O. Box 1
Cambridge, Massachusetts 02139
(617) 661-4090

Boston Area Rape Crisis Center
c/o Women's Center
46 Pleasant Street
Cambridge, Massachusetts 02139
(617) 492-RAPE

Greater Lynn Rape Task Force
c/o Lynn Economic Opportunity
360 Washington Street
Lynn, Massachusetts 01901

Springfield Rape Crisis Center, Inc.
292 Worthington Street, Room 215
Springfield, Massachusetts 01103
(413) 737-RAPE

Women's Intervention Center
Vineyard Haven, Massachusetts 02568

MICHIGAN

Women's Crisis Center
306 N. Division Street
Ann Arbor, Michigan 48108
(313) 994-9100

Women's Alternatives Crisis Center
203 15th Street
Bay City, Michigan 48706
(517) 892-1551

Detroit Rape Crisis Line
P.O. Box 35271
7 Oaks Station
Detroit, Michigan 48235
(313) 872-RAPE

Women Against Rape
2445 W. 8 Mile
Detroit, Michigan 48203
(313) 892-7161

Rape Crisis Team
Box 6161, Station C
Grand Rapids, Michigan 49506
(616) 774-3535

MINNESOTA

Rape Counseling Center
Neighborhood Involvement Program
2617 Hennepin Avenue
Minneapolis, Minnesota 55408
(612) 374-4357

Center for Rational Living
2130 Fairways Land
Roseville, Minnesota 55113
(612) 631-2046

Family Tree
1599 Selby Avenue
St. Paul, Minnesota 55104
(612) 645-0478

Minneapolis Program for Victims
430 Metro Sq. Building
St. Paul, Minnesota 55101

Sex Offense Services Committee
c/o Department of Social Work
St. Paul-Ramsey Hospital
St. Paul, Minnesota 55101
(612) 222-4260 (X-402)

MISSISSIPPI

Rape Counseling Service
P.O. Box 4902
Jackson, Mississippi 39216
(601) 354-1113

Rape Crisis Center
P.O. Box 2971
University City, Mississippi 63160
(314) 773-1313

MISSOURI

Metropolitan Organization to Counter
Sexual Assault
P.O. Box 15492
Kansas City, Missouri 64106

MONTANA

Rape Relief Program
Woman's Place
1130 W. Broadway
Missoula, Montana 59801
(406) 543-7606

NEBRASKA

Lincoln Coalition Against Rape
c/o Women's Resource Center
Room 116 Nebraska Union
University of Nebraska
Lincoln, Nebraska 68508
(402) 472-2597

NEVADA

Community Action Against Rape
1212 Casino Boulevard
Las Vegas, Nevada 89104
(702) 735-1111 (crisis)
(702) 385-0158 (office)

Rape Crisis Center
325 Flint Street
Reno, Nevada 89501
(702) 329-RAPE

NEW HAMPSHIRE

Women Against Rape
N.H. Women's Health Services
38 S. Main Street
Concord, New Hampshire 03301
(603) 225-2739

NEW JERSEY

Camden County Women Against Rape
P.O. Box 346
Collingwood, New Jersey 08108
(609) 662-3000

Bergen County Women Against Rape
P.O. Box 624
Englewood, New Jersey 07631
(201) 567-3289

Rape Crisis Center
7 State St.
Glassboro, New Jersey 08028
(609) 881-4040

Rape Survival Center
P.O. Box 1600
Hillside, New Jersey 07205
(201) 527-2450

Atlantic County Rape Crisis Center
P.O. Box 3058
Margate, New Jersey 08403
(609) 853-8300

Rape Crisis Intervention Center
P.O. Box 151
Metuchen, New Jersey 08840

Sexual Assault Rape Analysis
20 Park Pl.
Newark, New Jersey 07102
(201) 733-RAPE

Women's Crisis Center
56 College Avenue
New Brunswick, New Jersey 08901
(201) 828-RAPE

Mercer County Women Against Rape
103 W. Hanover Street
Trenton, New Jersey 08618
(609) 896-1045

Rape Action Center
P.O. Box 722
Willingboro, New Jersey 08046
(609) 871-4700

NEW MEXICO

Rape Crisis Center
1824 Las Lomas N.E.
Albuquerque, New Mexico 87131
(505) 277-3393

NEW YORK

Crime Victims Service Center
Center for the Study of Social Intervention
Albert Einstein College of Medicine
Ginsburg Building, Room 3-14
Bronx, New York 10461
(212) 829-5522

Anti-Rape and Sexual Assault Program
YWCA
190 Franklin Street
Buffalo, New York 14202
(716) 852-6120

Crisis Service
3258 Main Street
Buffalo, New York 14214
(716) 838-5980

Director of Education
Planned Parenthood
210 Franklin Street
Buffalo, New York 14202
(716) 853-1771

Erie County Anti-Rape and Sexual
Assault Program
95 Franklin Street, Room 1376

**Community
antirape
projects**

163

Buffalo, New York 14202
(716) 846-6462

Queens Women Against Rape
Queens College
Kissena Boulevard
Flushing, New York 11367

Crisis Intervention Center
C.W. Post Center
Long Island University
Greenvale, New York 11548
(516) 299-2575 (crisis)
(516) 299-2578 (office)

Mayor's Task Force on Rape
52 Chambers Street, Room 112
New York, New York 10017
(212) 566-0382

National Association of Junior Leagues
825 3rd Avenue
New York, New York 10022
(212) 355-4380

New York Women Against Rape
222 East 19th Street
New York, New York 10003
(212) 877-8700 (crisis)
(212) 477-0819 (office)

Rape Crisis Service
Planned Parenthood of Rochester and
Monroe County, Inc.
24 Windsor Street
Rochester, New York 14605
(716) 546-2595

NORTH CAROLINA

Chapel Hill-Carrboro Rape Crisis Center
P.O. Box 871
Chapel Hill, North Carolina 27514
(919) 967-RAPE

North Carolina Memorial Hospital
Emergency Room Rape Crisis Program
c/o Dept. of Psychiatry
School of Medicine
University of North Carolina
Chapel Hill, North Carolina 27514
(919) 966-4551

OHIO

Akron Women Against Rape
c/o Humanity House
475 W. Market Street
Akron, Ohio 44313
(216) 434-7273

Rape Crisis Center
Women Helping Women
2699 Clifton Avenue
Cincinnati, Ohio 45220

(513) 861-2959
(513) 861-8616

Rape Crisis Center
3201 Euclid Avenue
Cleveland, Ohio 44115
(216) 391-3912

Prosecutor's Office
41 N. Perry Street
Dayton, Ohio 45402
(513) 223-8085

Victimization Project
Ombudsman
Centre City Building, Suite 208
15 East 4th Street
Dayton, Ohio 45402
(513) 223-4613

Project Woman Rape Crisis Center
22 East Grand Avenue
Springfield, Ohio 45506
(513) 325-3707

Toledo United Against Rape
1831 W. Bancroft Street
Toledo, Ohio 43606
(419) 475-0494

OKLAHOMA

Oklahoma County YWCA Rape Crisis Center
YWCA Women's Resource Center
722 N.W. 30th
Oklahoma City, Oklahoma 73118
(405) 528-5508 (crisis)
(405) 528-5440 (office)

OREGON

Rape Prevention Center
P.O. Box 625
370½ W. 6th Street
Eugene, Oregon 97401
(503) 485-0234

Rape Relief Hotline
P.O. Box 1363
Portland, Oregon 97201
(503) 235-5333

Rape Victim Advocate Project
Multnomah County D.A.'s Office
600 County Court House
Portland, Oregon 97201
(503) 248-5059

Women's Crisis Service
Box 851
Salem, Oregon 97308
(503) 399-7722

PENNSYLVANIA

Harrisburg Area Rape Crisis Center
P.O. Box 38

164

Harrisburg, Pennsylvania 17108
(717) 238-7273

Mon Yough-Allegheny County
Rape Crisis Center
810 Walnut Street
McKeesport, Pennsylvania 15132
(412) 664-0788

Center for Rape Concern
Philadelphia General Hospital
Mills Building C-16
700 Civic Center Boulevard
Philadelphia, Pennsylvania 19104
(215) 823-7966

Women Organized Against Rape
P.O. Box 17374
Philadelphia, Pennsylvania 19105
(215) 823-7997

Pittsburgh Action Against Rape
932 Baldwin Street (rear)
Pittsburgh, Pennsylvania 15234
(412) 678-8895 (McKeesport)
(412) 765-2731 (Pittsburgh)

Department of University Safety
Police Services
Pennsylvania State University
University Park, Pennsylvania 16802
(814) 863-1111

Chester County Rape Crisis Council
P.O. Box 738
West Chester, Pennsylvania 19380
(215) 692-RAPE

RHODE ISLAND

Rhode Island Rape Crisis Center
324 Broad St.
Central Falls, Rhode Island 02863

Committee on Criminal Sex Offenses
c/o Women's Liberation Union of Rhode Island
P.O. Box 2302
Eastside Station
Providence, Rhode Island 02906

SOUTH CAROLINA

Greenville General Hospital
Greenville Hospital Systems
Mallard Street
Greenville, South Carolina 29602
(803) 242-8377

TENNESSEE

Knoxville Rape Crisis Center
1831 Melrose Avenue, S.W.
Knoxville, Tennessee 37916
(615) 522-RAPE
(615) 522-7273

TEXAS

Austin Rape Crisis Center
P.O. Box 2247
Austin, Texas 78701
(512) 472-RAPE

Dallas Women Against Rape
P.O. Box 12701
Dallas, Texas 75225
(214) 341-9400

Women Against Rape
Box 3334
El Paso, Texas 79923
(915) 545-1500

Fort Worth/Tarrant County Task Force on Rape
512 W. 4th Street
Fort Worth, Texas 76102
(817) 338-4211

Rape Treatment, Detection,
Prevention Program
City Health Department
1115 N. MacGregory, Rm. 206
Houston, Texas 77025
(713) 222-4261

San Antonio Rape Crisis Line
P.O. Box 28061
San Antonio, Texas 78228
(512) 433-1251
(512) 433-8282

VERMONT

Women Against Rape
P.O. Box 92
Burlington, Vermont 05402
(802) 863-1236

VIRGINIA

Northern Virginia Hotline
P.O. Box 187
Arlington, Virginia 22210
(703) 527-4077

Roanoke Rape Crisis Center
3515 Williamson Road
Roanoke, Virginia 24012
(703) 366-6030

WASHINGTON

Renton Rape Line
1525 North 4th Street
Renton, Washington 98055
(206) 235-2315

Feminist Coordinating Council
5649 11th N.E.
Seattle, Washington 98105
(206) 325-8258

**Community
antirape
projects**

Community antirape projects

Rape Relief
4224 University Way, N.E.
Seattle, Washington 98105
(206) 632-RAPE

Sexual Assault Center
Harborview Medical Center
325 Ninth Avenue
Seattle, Washington 98104
(206) 223-3010 (nights and weekends)
(206) 223-3047 (days)

Rape Crisis Network
N. 507 Howard
Spokane, Washington 99201
(509) 624-7273

WISCONSIN

Dane County Project on Rape
120 W. Mifflin Street
Madison, Wisconsin 53703
(608) 251-5440

Rape Crisis Center
P.O. Box 1312
Madison, Wisconsin 53701
(608) 251-RAPE

Wisconsin Task Force on Rape
2770 N. 44th Street
Milwaukee, Wisconsin 53210

Witness Support/Anti-Rape Unit
Office of the District Attorney

Room 206, Safety Building
Milwaukee, Wisconsin 53208
(414) 278-4617

CANADA

Rape Relief
1027 West Broadway
Vancouver, British Columbia
Canada V6H1E2
(604) 732-1613

Toronto Rape Crisis Centre
Box 6597
Postal Station A
Toronto, Ontario
Canada M5W1X4
(416) 368-8383 (crisis)
(416) 368-5695 (office)

AUSTRALIA

Women Against Rape
85 Johnston Street
Collingwood, Victoria
Australia 3006
419-4644

Women's House
25 Alberta Street
Sydney, New South Wales
Australia
617-325

SELECTED BIBLIOGRAPHY

Adleman, Connie, R.N., and Johnson, Margaret, R.N. *Trainex Nursing Audio Journal* (cassette training for nurses). Trainex Corporation, Garden Grove, Calif., 1976.

Burgess, Ann Wolbert, R.N., and Holmstrom, Lynda Lytle. *Rape: Victims of Crisis*. Bowie, Md.: Robert J. Brady, 1974.

Burgess, Ann Wolbert, R.N., and Holmstrom, Lynda Lytle. "Sexual Assault: Signs and Symptoms." *Journal of Emergency Nursing,* March-April 1976, pp. 11-16.

Burgess, Ann Wolbert, R.N., and Holmstrom, Lynda Lytle. "The Rape Victim in the Emergency Room." *American Journal of Nursing,* 73: 1741-1745.

Copeland, L., and Norlin, L. "Examination and Treatment of Victims of Sexual Assault." *San Francisco Medicine,* June, 1976, pp. 18-21.

"District of Columbia City Council Memorandum." Washington, D.C.: Public Safety Committee Task Force on Rape, 1973.

Evrard, John R. "Rape: The Medical, Social and Legal Implications." *American Journal of Obstetrics and Gynecology* 111: 197-199.

Fox, Sandra S., and Scherl, Donald J., M.D. "Crisis Intervention With Victims of Rape." *Social Work* 17: 37-42.

Gill, Sally, R.N. "Victims of Sexual Assault." *Imprint,* December, 1975, pp. 24-33.

Selected bibliography

Graves, L.R., M.D., and Francisco, T., M.D. "Medico-legal Aspects of Rape." *Medical Aspects of Human Sexuality*, April 1970, pp. 109-120.

"Guide to Medical Services Following Sexual Assault." New York City Mayor's Task Force on Rape.

Hayman, Charles R., M.D. "Roundtable: Rape and Its Consequences." *Medical Aspects of Human Sexuality*, February 1972, pp. 12-31.

Keefe, Mary, and O'Reilly, Henry. "Changing Perspectives in Sex Crimes Investigations." In *Sexual Assault: The Victim and the Rapist*. Lexington, Mass.: D.C. Heath and Co., 1976.

Keefe, Mary, and O'Reilly, Henry. "Rape: Attitudinal Training for Police and Emergency Room Personnel." *The Police Chief*, November 1975, pp. 36-37.

Keefe, Mary and O'Reilly, Henry. "The Plight of the Rape Victim in New York City." In *Victims and Society*, edited by Emilio Viano. Washington, D.C.: Visage Press, 1976.

Lichtenstein, Grace. "Rape Laws Undergoing Changes to Aid Victims." *New York Times*, 4 June, 1975, p. 1.

Masters, William H., M.D., and Johnson, Virginia E. "The Aftermath of Rape," *Redbook*, June 1976, p. 74.

McGuire, L.S., and Stern, Michael, M.S. "Survey of Incidence of and Physicians' Attitudes Toward Sexual Assault." *Public Health Reports* 91, 103-109.

Peters, Joseph J., M.D. "Child Rape: Defusing the Psychological Time Bomb." *Hospital Physician*, February 1973, pp. 46-49.

Peters, Joseph J., M.D. "The Psychological Aftereffects of Rape." *Contemporary OB/Gyn*, January 1976, pp. 105-108.

Rape and Its Victims: A Report for Citizens, Health Facilities, and Criminal Justice Agencies. 4 vols. Washington, D.C.: Center for Women's Policy Studies, 1974.

"Rape and Other Sexual Assaults—What to Expect After

the Attack." Pamphlet. Rockville, Md.: Montgomery
County Government Department of Police.

Robertson, Nan. "The Ordeal of Rape Is Eased by the
City's Sex Crime Unit." *New York Times*, 20 November 1976, p. 12.

Schultz, Leroy G., ed. *Rape Victimology*, Springfield, Illinois: Charles C Thomas, 1975.

Sutherland, S., and Scherl, D., M.D. "Patterns of Response Among Victims of Rape." *American Journal of Orthopsychiatry* 40: 503-511.

The Boston Women's Health Book Collective. *Our Bodies Ourselves*. New York: Simon and Schuster, 1973.

"Treating the Rape Victim." *Medical World News*, 8 March, 1976, pp. 50-58.

Zuspan, Frederick P., M.D., et al. "Alleged Rape: An Invitational Symposium." *The Journal of Reproductive Medicine* 12: 133-144, passim.